Sunderland at War

Sunderland
at War

Chaz Bowyer

L5798, DA-A of 210
Squadron leaves its
mooring for take-off, 1940.
First flown on September
1st, 1938, L5798 later served
as KC-B of 204 Squadron,
and ended its service in
October 1943 at Calshot
when it was ultimately
struck off RAF charge.

LONDON

IAN ALLAN LTD

Contents

First published 1976
Reprinted 1979

ISBN 0 7110 0665 2

Designed by Anthony Wirkus LSIA

Published by Ian Allan Ltd, Shepperton, Surrey;
and printed in the United Kingdom by
Ian Allan Printing Ltd

Introduction

The age of the flying boat in RAF history was a unique era. From 1912 until 1959 flying boats were a relatively small but vital section of the British flying services, allied directly to a centuries-old maritime tradition in the final decades of the British Empire with its far-flung territories and responsibilities. During those years over 100 different types of flying boats were designed for RAF use — none surpassed the Short Sunderland. It was not only the ultimate, but the queen of the 'boats. From the launching of the prototype until the final Sunderland flight carrying RAF livery, the Sunderland served for almost exactly 21 years — a longevity of front-line service virtually unmatched by any other RAF operational aircraft. To the lay mind, and probably to a majority of servicemen of the day, the Sunderland epitomised RAF Coastal Command during the 1939-45 war. From the first day of hostilities until final victory Sunderlands served long, well and splendidly; guarding merchant shipping lifelines to the United Kingdom, seeking out and destroying the wolves of the oceans, U-boats, acting as mercy vehicles, supply and communications craft, evacuating sorely-pressed troops from near-impossible situations.

To its crews the Sunderland was much more than just a good machine — it represented a wholly distinct way of life. As with no other aircraft used by the RAF, it became war chariot, home, bed and board to the men who flew it — a unique relationship 'twixt man and machine being firmly established from the very beginning. This affinity was admittedly aided and abetted by inherited traditions of the so-termed 'Flying Boat Union', that tight-knit community of all military flying boat crews with its highly esoteric way of life and attitudes. Operational seniority among those 'web-foot warriors' was outwardly evident in the depth of verdigris on a cap badge and tunic buttons; the near-naval terminology in everyday speech; and by no means least, an extraordinary close comradeship. On operations Sunderland captains enjoyed virtual autonomy of action, the very nature of their duties calling for individual decisions in peculiarly individual circumstances. Once airborne a Sunderland was literally a self-contained war unit of men and machine, with a breadth of possible situations and actions unknown to any landplane. Perhaps that self-sufficiency is best and simplest illustrated by the fact that it was not uncommon for crews between operational sorties to live aboard their aircraft, rather than revert to the normal Service domesticity of mess, bunk and billet. As with the vast majority of Coastal Command, Sunderland crews led a frustrating existence throughout the war in the context of actual contact with an enemy. It was no exception for a crew to spend hundreds of hours flying operationally without even seeing a U-boat, let alone attacking and/or destroying one. The succinct summation of his war career by Wing Commander L. G. J. Archambault, AFC, wartime commander of 423 Squadron, RCAF, was 'I flew like a son-of-a-gun, never saw anything, never shot at anything, nobody ever shot at me, not even my friends, and I never saw a German' — a sentiment probably echoed by a large majority of other ex-Sunderland men. Post-war German records confirm that Sunderlands were responsible for sinking 37 U-boats, probably sinking two, and seriously damaging 19 others. This tally does not take into account the far greater number of underwater killers attacked, forced to submerge and thereby effectively deterred from attacking Allied shipping. It was in this 'air deterrent' role that the Sunderland made its greatest overall contribution to the sea/air war. No statistics can be compiled to calculate the many thousands of lives and millions of tons of vital supplies that were spared the attentions of enemy submarines due directly to the ever-present air escort.

The background to the Sunderland story started in November 1933, in which month Air Ministry issued AM Specification R.2/33 calling for a four-engined, long-range, general purpose flying boat to succeed the various biplane 'boats then equipping RAF Coastal units. No specific requirement was stated for a monoplane configuration but Short Brothers, the original pioneers of British aircraft manufacturers and the most experienced firm in the field of maritime aircraft design, decided to produce a militarised equivalent of a parallel project civil flying boat then being produced for Imperial Airways, the C-Class, or as it became popularly known, Empire Class. The first C-Class, *Canopus,* was launched on July 2nd, 1936; a year later, on October 16th, 1937, the prototype Sunderland, K4774, made its first brief flight at Rochester, Kent, with that doyen of flying boat pilots, John Parker, at the controls. The first Sunderland to enter RAF service was L2159 which was collected by a 210 Squadron crew on May 28th, 1938 and flown to Seletar, Singapore, arriving there on June 22nd and being handed over to 230 Squadron. By October 1938, 230 Squadron had fully re-equipped, having eight Sunderlands on charge. In the UK, 210 Squadron received its first pair of Sunderlands, L2162 and L2163, on June 24th 1938, and by September 1939 had six on strength; while the only other pre-war unit to

be Sunderland-equipped, 204 at Mount Batten, began receiving their aircraft in July 1939. By August 1945 a total of 20 squadrons had employed Sunderlands, and production finally ceased on June 14th, 1946. The post-war career of the Sunderland, and its civil variations, are not strictly within the compass of this book, but it should be realised that in RAF use the Sunderland continued to give splendid service in many waters. It participated in the Berlin Air Lift, Malayan Emergency, Korean War, and numerous minor operations until May 20th, 1959, when ML797 of 205 Squadron, Seletar made the ultimate RAF Sunderland flight bearing RAF roundels. It was the swan song not only of the Sunderland, but of all RAF flying boats.

The path to the final assembly of text and illustrations for this Sunderland panorama was considerably smoothed by unselfish and willing help from many friends and fellow aviation 'knuts'. Not least was the spontaneous generosity and co-operation of a wide nunber of ex-Sunderland crew members, air and ground, whose abiding affection for their aircraft was only too obvious in the correspondence and interviews we held. To list every name would appear invidious — some insisted on anonymity — therefore may I offer an open hand of sincere gratitude for their aid and valued encouragement. They will know whom I mean — I can only hope this book meets with their approval. If in addition the contents give a younger generation even a slight insight into the contemporary conditions, and especially the sacrifices made by Sunderland crews during the years 1939-1945, it will have achieved its main purpose.

Norwich 1975   CHAZ BOWYER

Pedigree

Short Singapore III, K3592, the last operational military biplane 'boat produced by Short Brothers, seen here 'on the step' at take-off from the Medway on July 26th, 1934. It represented an accumulation of practical experience in marine aircraft design by the parent firm over a period of 21 years.

Right: *Satyrus* — Short S.17 Kent, G-ABFC of the Imperial Airways Fleet, which was launched on April 30th, 1930, and served staunchly until being finally scrapped at Hythe in June 1938.

Below: QUEEN MOTHER. The prototype Short Sunderland, K4774, poised on the slipway at Short Bros' Rochester works. Its first flight took place on October 16th, 1937.

Bottom: A second aspect of the first-ever Sunderland, its pristine sheen reflecting the dull sunshine, and emphasising the bulky beauty of the design.

Left: STABLE-MATE. Short S.23 C-Class (Empire) civil air liner *Cavalier* (G-ADUU) of Imperial Airways. Its parallel production to the Sunderland inspired many basic features in the latter design. This particular flying boat was finally lost at sea on January 21st, 1939 during a routine trans-Atlantic run.

Below: An almost perfect head-on view of the Sunderland prototype.

Right: TRIALS. L2160, the third production Sunderland I, flying over Walton Battery on the Orwell, Felixstowe on June 3rd, 1938 during fuel jettison trials by the RAF. Shortly after L2160 was flown to 230 Squadron at Seletar, Singapore, arriving there on July 4th.

L2160, now on charge to 230 Squadron, being 'christened' *Selangor* by the Sultan of that State, at Port Swettenham, October 1938. Of the squadron's full strength of eight Sunderlands then, two other aircraft were similarly named *Pahang* and *Perak*.

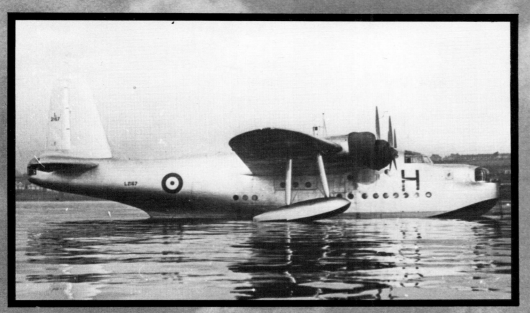

Left: H-HARRY. L2167, first launched at Rochester on July 27th, 1938, seen in pre-war finish, on strength of 210 Squadron.

Left: PARKING PROBLEM. The massive proportions of a Sunderland tail presented awkward storage in normal sized hangars — as readily shown here by the *derriére* of L5805. Later, L5805 was allotted to 95 Squadron and flew the unit's first war operation. It then served with 228 Squadron, and eventually became Y-Yorker of 201 Squadron.

Right: AIRBORNE. L5806 which served initially with 10 Squadron RAAF and, in April 1940, was on charge of 228 Squadron.

Below left: Another view of L5806 in its normal environment.

Below right: FRIENDLY FOURSOME. A peaceful pre-war scene of Sunderlands in formation skirting the Sussex coastline near Littlehampton. Nearest machine is L5806.

First Impressions
Ron Codd

MESSING ABOUT IN BOATS. Groundcrew in a pinnace installing beaching legs on the starboard side of Sunderland III, ML774, '2-F' of 422 Squadron RCAF at Pembroke Dock, December 8th, 1944. Note retracted nose turret in moored position and the two side vents on the nose side which housed two of the four fixed ·50 machine guns installed as extra forward armament by that stage of the war.

Left: BEACHED. The sheer bulk of a Sunderland fuselage 'scaled' by the two airmen here. Scene at Pembroke Dock, 1939.

Below left: The cavernous interior of a Sunderland I, looking forward — a luxury in space part-inherited from its civil stable-mate, the C-Class 'boat.

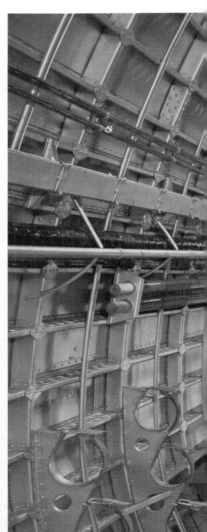

The first encounter I had with a Sunderland was in a hangar where, minus its mainplane and draped with safety nets, it rested on concrete blocks and its beaching gear. This aircraft was used as an aircrew familiarisation machine and was our introduction to working as a crew. Its vast bulk inside the hangar was most impressive, and coming as I had from Ansons and Oxfords the interior was cavernous. This awe of its sheer size never left me throughout my aircrew service in her and, I feel, created my strong affection for the aircraft. A typical operational patrol would begin with perhaps a call in the early hours of the morning and, after struggling into flying kit, a short trudge from the billet to the aircrew mess where the customary bacon and eggs could, at times, be enough to turn the strongest stomach. After collecting flying rations, a visit next to the briefing room to gather details of the patrol, intelligence, signals and weather forecast. Next stop was the jetty to board a dinghy or pinnace to ferry us to our aircraft. The stench of diesel fuel from these boats is another vivid impression that has remained with me ever since — one I'm sure I share with quite a few Sunderland aircrews. On clambering aboard through the front door, we dispersed to our various duties to carry out pre-flight checks on our equipment.

The choice of patrol, weather conditions en route, time of day over the operational area explained to us at briefing could be a nail-biting experience. It could happen that we would be making for the Spanish coast, cruising at about 110 knots in brilliant sunshine and a cloudless sky — with a resultant twitch in one's system at the prospect of meeting German fighters in decidedly unfavourable circumstances. At the other extreme were the patrols carried out in stormy and turbulent conditions, flying fairly low down over the sea for several hours, with all the physical discomfort and air sickness that accompanied such conditions. Nevertheless, take-off in a Sunderland was to me always a thrilling experience. Standing between the two pilots one saw the control column pulled back and the bows come up as the throttles were eased forward in pairs. The spray being pounded from the hull, the floats skimming the water and finally the boat lifting majestically to the roar of its engines. It never failed to excite me. A night take-off, with full petrol and bomb load, was a much more protracted affair which often seemed interminable before coming unstuck.

Below: The same view taken from slightly further back. The ladder (left) led up to the midships hatches and (centre) the flight deck.

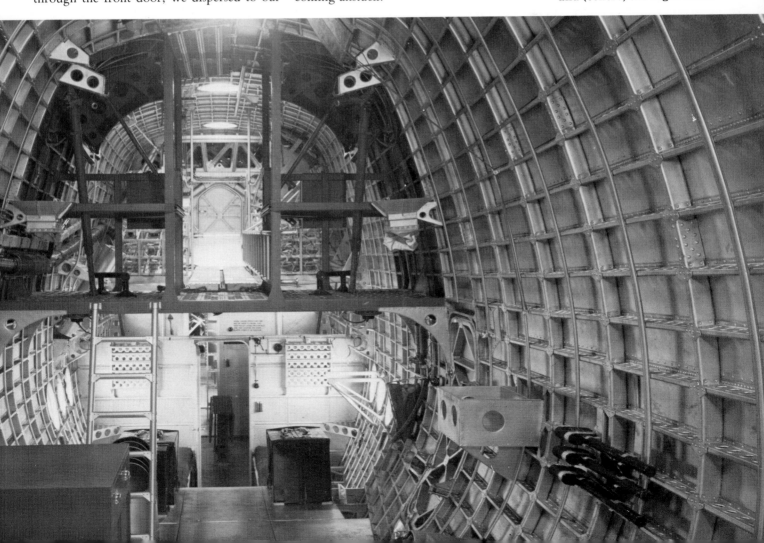

To be in the bows on a black cold and windy night, with a rough sea running, trying to remove the anchor chains from the buoy and get the aircraft onto a short rope slip prior to a night take-off was to me the very height of discomfort. Apart from distinctly nauseous stirrings in one's stomach at times, there was the physical activity involved in unloosening shackle pins with frozen hands, or holding the Aldis lamp in a suitable position for illumination, followed by the stowing of the mooring bollard and winding forward of the nose turret once we had slipped our moorings. At night the take-off was always some miles away from our base, where a flarepath was laid consisting of a control pinnace and several small lights laid out in one line, take-off and landings being made to the starboard side of these lights. Preparations for a night take-off were always pretty tiring as the aircraft had to be towed to take-off point during the day, thus requiring a duty crew to be aboard during this time.

Sitting in the mid-upper turret at night, slowly revolving in search sweeps, could be a peculiar sensation. One felt quite detached when there were long periods of silence over the intercom, broken occasionally by another crew member switching on his microphone and blowing into it, as if to reassure himself that he was not alone. One could plainly see the blue glow from flame-dampened exhaust pipes, and a faint light from the navigator's and radio operator's stations reflected through the astro-dome. This was a first class look-out position with a view right forward over the

Later modifications led to simplification of the original Mk I's dorsal gun hatches, these being replaced (as here) by two side-fuselage hatches, each providing a fire-point for a hand-fired ·50 machine gun. Note the pair of oars stowed at left.

Below: BRIDGE. The skipper and 1st Pilot's seats on the flight deck or 'bridge'. Near left is the wireless operator's desk and gear; while at right can be seen a corner of the navigator's chart table.

Above: DEFENCE. A Sunderland I's dorsal gunners' hatches. At left an air gunner stands by his single ·303 VGO gun; while at right a crew member is using an F.42 hand camera through the gunner's hatchway opening.

Above centre: BOMB AIMER. In the lower nose section of a Sunderland I of 10 Squadron RAAF, early 1940. At bottom left can be seen the anchor stowage; while centre right is the head of the indispensable boat hook.

Above right: HARRY FLAKERS — one of the bunks for 'off-duty' crew men, just below the port waist gun platform.

Right: STEAK ALFRESCO. An LAC air gunner does double duty as chief cook and bottle-washer, preparing fried steak and the inevitable potatoes for the crew on a primus stove. The somewhat herculean size and weight of RAF issue cooking utensils kept Sunderland crew 'chefs' in muscle trim, if nothing else . . .

Far right: BEANS, BEANS, BEANS . . . but apparently much appreciated here as Sergeant Doug Meaney hands a plateful to Sergeant Jack Shand, an air gunner, aboard a Sunderland III of 423 Squadron RCAF, April 6th, 1943.

22

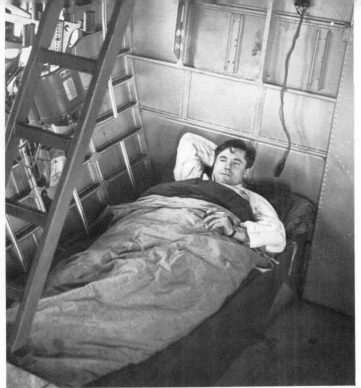

bows and to port and starboard, broken only by the expanse of wing. On being relieved from duty in the mid-upper, signified by a tug on the legs, one could either climb down a flight of steps at the rear of the bomb bay, or regain the flight deck by going through a small door into the flight engineer's position, the opening of which produced a blast of cold air mingled with a compounded smell of petrol, rubber and, often, the results of cooking in the galley. On one night patrol, after the radar operator had picked up a contact, the captain homed onto the target and lost height for his attack. Bomb doors were pulled down, but the bomb racks did not extend fully to the dropping position. In a frantic rush two crew members groped their way upstairs to use the hand winding gear forward of the midships turret. In the light of our flares, and with the bomb racks not yet fully out, we saw our target clearly — a whale!

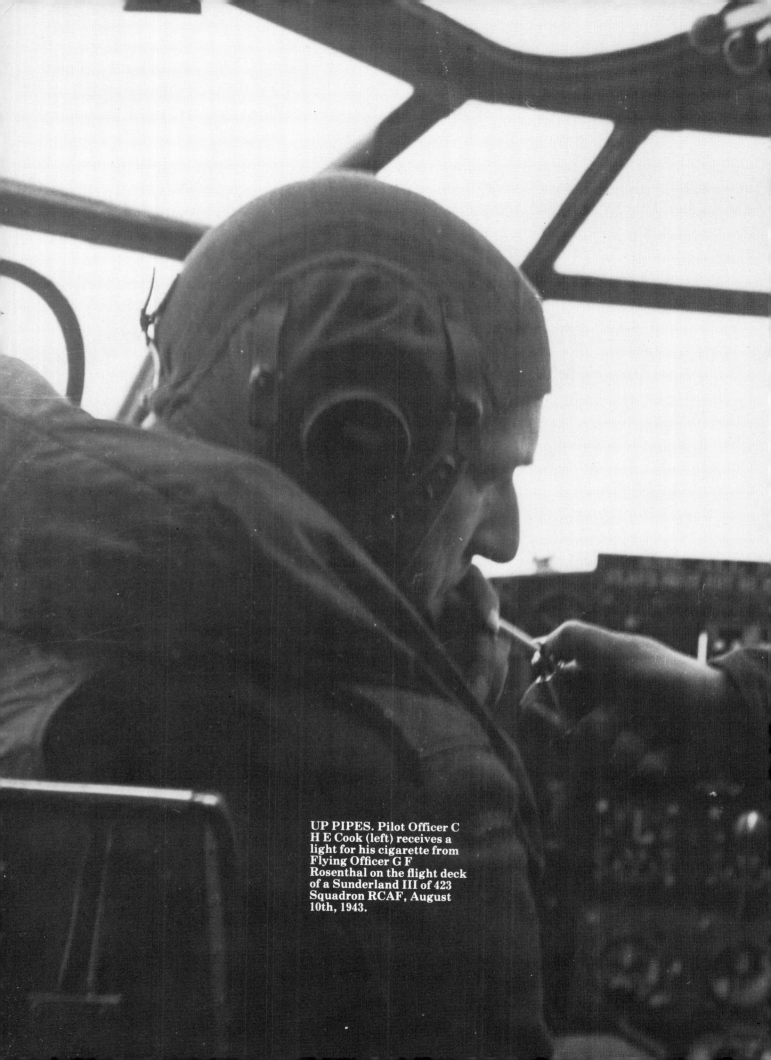

UP PIPES. Pilot Officer C H E Cook (left) receives a light for his cigarette from Flying Officer G F Rosenthal on the flight deck of a Sunderland III of 423 Squadron RCAF, August 10th, 1943.

Skipper's View

Vic Hodgkinson, Australian-born, joined the RAAF in late 1938 and, after pilot training, joined 10 (RAAF) Squadron on March 10, 1940. For the next two years he flew Sunderlands on operations in which period he accumulated just over 1800 hours flying, and was awarded a DFC. Returning to Australia in mid-1942, he successively commanded Nos 20 and 40 Squadrons, RAAF — again on flying boats (Catalinas). After the war he returned to England and joined BOAC, flying civil versions of the Sunderland until 1950, by which time he had logged some 7,500 hours on flying boats of all types. During the early years, 1940-42, his operational experiences were fairly typical of a majority of Sunderland skippers — long, monotonous hours of 'watching water', with few contacts with any enemy, and fewer 'eyeball' encounters with the arch-enemies, U-boats. This is not to say that his operational career was without incident or danger. With all the inherent, awesome 'opposition' of weather and ocean, flying boat crews had enough natural enemies with which to contend — U-boats and the Luftwaffe merely added to their daily risks.

'I think the thing that impressed me most was first on approaching and seeing this enormous slab-sided monster. Then once inside still being impressed by the amount of space, and the height of the flight deck off the water. On touch-down one was even further off the water. . . Start-up was a fairly simple procedure. Once on board normal checks were carried out, the 'rake' was removed (this locked the flying controls with — normally — the elevator in the down position, stick forward), and flying controls checked for freedom of movement. Exactors were bled, making sure that fuel cocks were 'Off', otherwise fuel would be injected into the carbs and could cause a fire on start-up. Check on short slip (storm pennant stowed); check lay of aircraft on the buoy to wind direction, and current position of the aircraft in relation to other aircraft, obstacles etc. With fuel cocks 'On', give the engineer the order of starting engines so that he could prime them. Generally, port outer was opened first to bring the buoy on the port side, so that the captain could keep it in view; or starboard outer, depending on the way the aircraft was laying. The use of drogues in this position to help turn the aircraft would have more than likely fouled the buoy. With the two outers running, slip the moorings — the

POWER. The starboard engines, props and float, as viewed from the right-hand (1st Pilot's) seat, in flight. A common legend among Sunderland pilots was that any failure of the inboard prop usually meant either decapitation in the cockpit, or the loss of the outboard prop as well.

Above: TEA BREAK. Flight Lieutenant Vic Hodgkinson, DFC, skippering a 10 Squadron RAAF Sunderland, pauses for the periodic 'cuppa' during a patrol.

Above right: Two views of the skipper's seat and dashboard in a Sunderland I. The control stick wheel was a natural adaption in design from the familiar automobile driver's wheel of the period.

Right: AUSSIES IN EXILE. Some of the first crew members of 10 Squadron RAAF, Pembroke Dock, 1940. From left: Doug Crockford; Stan ('The Count') Goddard; Bob Smith; Jack ('Astro') Jewell; Tom ('Lofty') Jensen; Stan Nicholls; Ted Cock and Jack Lanyon. This unit became officially operational on February 1st, 1940, and flew its first official squadron operation on the 6th; although its aircrews had been part-operational for some months before

signal given to the crew member in the bow was by whistle, hand signals or a shout. Start up inners when clear of the moorings — again, order of selection depended on wind direction. All hatches, bow turret (with bollard stowed) closed, except when using the drogues to help turn or take the way off the aircraft in a confined space, when the galley hatches would be open — drogues were operated from this position.

Once you were taxying there was no stopping or reversing, so you had to think ahead and avoid any 'tight' position. It was generally said that on flying boats 'all troubles started once you were on the water.' The signals for the drogues were three lights — red, white and green with switches — on the starboard instrument panel, and another set in the galley. White gave 'stand-by' warning accompanied by a klaxon, also used for alarum to alert crews to action stations. Turning on the water in reasonable conditions could be accomplished by use of the outer engines, sometimes assisted by the adjoining inner. In conditions of strong winds all the stops had to be pulled out by swinging the

aircraft first in the opposite direction, using engines, aileron and rudder; then belting the other outer and setting the flying controls in the opposite sense to help bring it to a down-wind direction. As it approached the down-wind direction you had to stop the swing by using the other outer, and control it also by use of rudder and ailerons, otherwise it would weathercock back into wind. The use of flying controls was — opposite aileron, some rudder into wind and same aileron, opposite rudder down-wind. Engine run-up with a load up was in pairs — outers and inners; but when lightly laden all four could be run up together.

Take-off.

Fine pitch — flaps one third — hatches closed — elevator 0-2 degrees, nose up — stick back and aileron and rudder applied according to wind direction. In rough conditions it was necessary to keep the floats clear of the waves, a little wing-down into wind to help keep the aircraft straight; wing-up into wind could give you an uncontrollable water loop and possible loss of a

29

float. Opening up engines again depended on conditions. A straightforward take-off into wind, heavily laden, required the outers to be opened first adjusting these with flying controls to keep the aircraft straight; then opening the inners slowly, trying to avoid the props hitting the bow wave spray. Crosswind take-off required opening the two outers to get the aircraft running straight with the up-wind engine fully open, and the down-wind engine anywhere from closed to threequarters-open. Follow up with the inners until fully open and, as rudder control was established, the retarded outer was gradually opened up. This seemed the ideal but it still needed a lot of juggling and anticipation. It was a case of 'suck it and see'. In good conditions, and lightly laden, all four could be opened up together. As the aircraft came up onto the step the stick was eased to the central position and the aircraft allowed to plane and gain speed. When flying speed was attained the stick was eased back and the aircraft flown off the water. In rough seas, es-

pecially in swell conditions, the problem was to keep the boat on the water and in a planing attitude until sufficient flying speed could be attained. One could be thrown into the air quite a few times in these conditions, returning each time with a resounding thump. The main thing was to ease the aircraft back onto the water again and get it back into the planing attitude. Nose-up and you were in a good position to be thrown into the air again; while nose-down meant straight into the next green one and possible damage.

Another problem was porpoising i.e. pitching of the aircraft fore and aft. The cure for this was not to try to correct the attitude by applying opposite elevators — this was fatal because one was always one step behind and this merely made it worse — but by pulling the stick hard back and holding it there until the aircraft settled down; then easing it back to the planing attitude. If porpoising commenced before gaining elevator control then the only action to take was throttle back and start all over again. As the floats were considered the weak point on all Sunderlands, it was imperative to keep them clear of any rough seas. Apparently, when the aircraft was designed the various sections were handed out to different people to work on, and the bloke at Shorts whose job was to

Left: PIONEER. P9605, 'K' of 10 Squadron RAAF — the first Australian flying boat to fly an operational sortie during WW2. In early 1943 it was in use at 4(C) OTU as an instructional aircraft.

Below left: P9604, RB-J of 10 Squadron RAAF preparing to get away.

do the floats was not told, or didn't realise, that the wing flexed. The result was a large float attached to the flexible wing tip by two rigid struts and four very tight bracing wires. Another peculiar thing about the Sunderland was that all engines pointed *outwards*. What happened there was that the main plane (which was basically that of the C-Class flying boat) was first installed, and then it was found that with the tail turret the C of G was aft of that calculated. So instead of repositioning the main plane further back, the wing was kinked back from the hull. The engine nacelles were never altered to line up with the direction of flight — and therefore we had four built-in 'head-winds'. There was probably one saving grace, however — it helped in control of the aircraft when one had an outer engine failure.

Once in the air, with sufficient speed, throttle back to climb-boost, Mk I Sunderlands' variable pitch airscrews to coarse pitch; Mks II & III back to 2300 rpm. Level out, gain climb speed and climb away. At a safe height retract flaps — the beauty of the Gouge flaps was that no matter what the flap selection there was little or no elevator trim required.

In the air

The aircraft in the air was a dream to fly — very stable (probably due to the high wing) and the deep hull giving no pendulum effect. Ailerons and elevators were light finger-tip control, and the rudder a little heavier; though as with most heavy aircraft in the air this latter was not used much. We normally cruised at (I think) 120 knots, and around 1,000 feet mark. Synchronising engines was done by setting up the two inners by ear — then looking along the props and adjusting the outers until the 'shadows' stopped. The Aldis lamp was sometimes used for this purpose by night. I flew the Marks I, II and III Sunderlands and there was no difference between any of them from the flying point of view. If you could call it a difference then engine handling was the only one. The Mk I had vp airscrews and the following marks constant speed units (csu's); while the Pratt & Whitney Mk V had feathering props. The Pegasus was a very reliable and robust

Left: EN ROUTE. P9600, RB-E of 10 Squadron RAAF, snapped through a waist hatchway of its patrol companion, 1940, heading west over the Atlantic to rendezvous with a convoy. P9600 also served as DQ-T in 228 Squadron and ended its career as an instruction hack with 4(C) OTU in 1943.

Below left: X for X-RAY. RB-X of 10 Squadron RAAF flying over the Bristol Channel, heading for the sea. The dorsal gun turret, plus various radar antenae are evident.

ON THE BUOY. A 201 Squadron Sunderland resting on peaceful waters at Castle Archadale, N. Ireland. The aircraft's anchor chain and grabbit line (which was attached to the underwater bridles connected to the buoy) can be seen in this view.

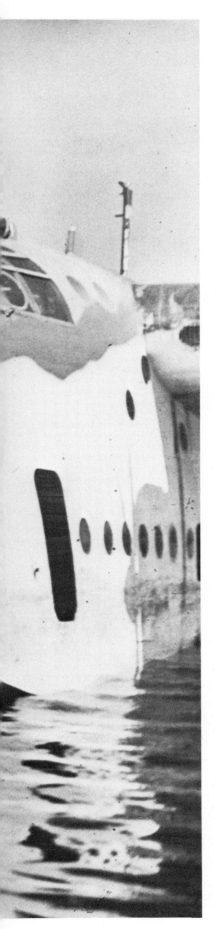

engine, although antiquated compared with the P & W R1830. I didn't fly the Mk V as such, but flew the Plymouth (Sandringham) version in BOAC for many years; and it handled the same as the Mks I, II & III. The Pratt & Whitney was an excellent engine (I flew 1800 hours on Catalinas fitted with these engines) and, what's more, it had feathering props, which none of the Pegasus engines had. I believe that it was not fitted because someone at Air Ministry said that it was not necessary on the Sunderland as they hadn't lost one due to engine failure..! The P & W didn't like being belted when cold. The bore in the cylinders was tapered, so that when hot the cylinder walls would be parallel; and if the engine was opened up cold there was a good chance of leaving a piston stuck in the top of a cylinder. Also we found in BOAC that the P & W installation in the Plymouth (Sandringham) overheated (cylinder head and oil) in very hot climates — probably due to poor airflow through the engine due to the larger engine nacelles which were designed for the Pegasus. Still, it was an excellent engine.

Patrol

When on patrol with the Mk I, the 450lb naval depth charges (dc's) were wound out by hand and the electrical connections made. In the Mk II's the depth charges were kept stored inboard and were operated from the pilot's seat by a lever which released the bomb doors, which in turn tripped a switch. This started an electric motor which wound out the bomb trolleys. With the Mk I we had two problems. One was the drag set up by four unstreamlined dc's hung out on the wing most of the time; and the second problem was after the dc's were out and the bomb doors closed, the armourer would then connect the electrics. Due to short circuiting et al one or more of the dc's would be released and lost. Above 100 feet and up to 500 feet when this happened the dc's would explode on hitting the surface of the water, and there'd be a violent kick up the back of the aircraft. At night there'd be an enormous flash of light to let you know that another 450lb of TNT had reached Mother Earth or sea. Operationally, these dc's had to be dropped as low and slow as possible.

Navigation was by DR day and night, using the drift-sight and tail turret to line up on white caps, smoke or flame floats. Astro-nav was seldom used. The marine sextant was not very reliable for day use, and the bubble sex-

tant didn't come into general use until late 1940. In any case, the weather was usually murky and one seldom saw the stars. We were equipped with ASV radar but this was fairly primitive and, as it was 'Secret' equipment, no one told us what it was capable of picking up. Some said that it would locate submarines under the surface, and we spent hours chasing blips in the empty ocean — which were probably faults in the set or extra large waves. It was good for picking up land masses and, later, responder beacons — when they materialised. Calling for radio bearings was taboo as we were on radio silence. In any case, we weren't told the locations of the DF stations.

Landing and mooring-up

In the circuit — fine pitch for vp airscrews on Mk I's; 2300 rpm for Mks II & III — third flap. When lined up, full flap and throttle back. Normally a glide approach and landing were carried out in daytime, but at night a powered and flatter approach was used. Drift was taken off either by nosing into wind or using the wing-down technique. Sunderlands could also be side-slipped to kick off surplus height. The aircraft was checked at about 20 feet and flown onto the water in the planing attitude. If too slow and the aircraft stalled you'd start a series of grinding bounces. Glossy calm or hazy conditions required a night landing technique i.e. powered flight and flat approach, as it was extremely difficult to see the surface. Also in very calm conditions a nose-down attitude was allowed to develop, and the aircraft would become uncontrollable and you'd finish up in a water loop and probably lose a float. Result — all hands out onto the wing with the good float and scream for the crash tender — *most* undignified! As the aircraft lost way the stick was eased back, and when the aircraft came off the step — which it did in a nose-up attitude — the stick had to be held hard back. If this wasn't done one would experience the stick thumping violently back due to the high speed jet of water from the step hitting the elevators. This could be reduced a little by applying some power on the inners as the aircraft came off the step. Once safely down, taxying was as before. Approaching the buoy was according to the wind state, tide, current and other obstacles. A good indication on how to approach the buoy was by observing the lay of other aircraft on the 'trots'. Even so, it was always a challenge and no two approaches were ever the same. If you missed

Right: MOORING — THE HARD WAY. A cartoon version of the everyday procedure of mooring a Sunderland, as seen through the eyes (and pen) of Wing Commander E G Oakley-Beauttler.

Above: AUSSIE SKIPPERS. Squadron Leader Smith (left) and Wing Commander V A Hodgkinson, DFC, RAAF in early 1945 when the latter commanded 40 Squadron RAAF, the only Sunderland unit based in Australian waters.

Above right: BOAT BASE. Air view of the well-used flying boat base at Oban, Scotland. It was never a popular base from an operational viewpoint, being almost constantly blanked out by low cloud and fog by night; while winter seas usually prohibited night flying.

the buoy and had to go round again, you were expected to buy a round of drinks for the crew. Approach to the buoy was made with full flap, inner engines cut, drogues streamed either singly to help turn or keep the aircraft's head in a certain direction, or both drogues. The buoy was brought up to the port side of the bow, where the crew member doing the acrobatic act was situated — hanging from the ladder with the short slip rope in one hand ready to slip it through the harness of the buoy, and the other hand and legs gripping the ladder. The problem was to pass it through the buoy harness — about one foot above the water — catch it as it went through, and then up the ladder with this end and make it fast to the bollard. The aircraft was then put back on the storm pennant etc and flaps retracted.

Night ops

The Aldis lamp was normally used as a searchlight when taxying at night, either from the bow or '2nd Dicky's' window. The

well down-wind before commencing one's run-up.

d) Using aircraft at moorings, where aircraft were moored in a line as in a river, and a flare path could be made by switching on all nav lights.

As with any large aircraft, the Sunderland had its minor technical problems. The hydraulic exactor throttle controls always gave trouble and required constant bleeding. In some aircraft on long patrols we used to resort to sending one of the engineers into the wing (a tight squeeze) to set and lock the throttle behind the engine. The APU (auxiliary power unit) was supposed to be for three-fold use — generating electricity, pumping fuel for refuelling the tanks, and bilging the aircraft. This was situated in the starboard leading edge and was a most unreliable unit. Another problem concerned the self-sealing petrol pipes. These were composed of a rubber substance which when fractured by a bullet would seal up and so prevent fuel loss. Unfortunately the connections sometimes leaked and the escaping fuel would seal up the pipe — resulting in the end of that engine for the remainder of the flight. The forward hatch, between the pilots' seats, was also a menace. Many a time I've got out of my seat and stepped into space — someone had left it open! Many 10 Squadron crews lived on board between trips. They had all they needed in the way of creature comforts, including a galley equipped with two primus stoves. It was quite common after fuelling up for some of the petrol to flow down the wing into the bilges; and for the crews — not to be deterred — to get the stoves going (accompanies by the usual starting-up flames from the primus) in this explosive atmosphere for a quick 'cuppa'. I never heard of one Sunderland catching fire from this source, however. All crews were very proud of their cutlery and crockery — 'borrowed' for the duration from various cafes, hotels and the like — and an example of this pride was on July 12, 1940. We were on a recce of St Nazaire and Bordeaux, looking for invasion barges, flying at 4,000 feet over Bordeaux; when the rigger who was setting up lunch in the wardroom burst onto the flight deck, complaining bitterly that a bullet had come up through the hull, through the table, and smashed his glass sugar bowl . . ! Other 'comforts' included a flush lavatory, wash basin, mirror, bunks, and even a lock-up cash box fitted in the ward room.

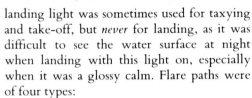

landing light was sometimes used for taxying and take-off, but *never* for landing, as it was difficult to see the water surface at night when landing with this light on, especially when it was a glossy calm. Flare paths were of four types:

a) Three lighted buoys — originally kerosene flares or, later, electric lights attached to an anchored buoy; the crash tender (always in attendance) making up the half-T.
b) Three lighted boats, generally used in open water. The boats would proceed slowly into wind, suitably spaced out, the leading boat lined up with the centre boat for wind direction etc., and the last boat lining up on these two.
c) Fixed flare path (as at Kalafrana, Malta). From a permanent buoy in the middle of the bay was attached, by a rope, a number of either electric or kerosene flares. These naturally streamed down-wind. This was a very short flare path and one needed to get

On the Panel

PENCIL AND PLOT.
Flying Officer Jack Ritchie,
a navigator, lays out his
chart-table. 423 Squadron
RCAF, August 10th, 1943.

Above left: ANY MORE FOR THE SKYLARK. A complete Sunderland crew of 422 Squadron RCAF waiting on a jetty to be borne to their aircraft. Back row, from left: Fg Off N C Rowley; Fg Off S Jones; Fg Off C H E Cook; Fg Off J D Graham; WO2 T E Campbell; Flt Sgt H J C Walerk; WO1 J O Fink and Fg Off T A Reeves. In front: Fg Off W J Bice; Fg Off W C Schmidt and Fg Off Fred Field. Pembroke Dock, December 8th, 1944.

Above Centre: CHECKING. Sergeant Leo Needham, a flight engineer, goes through his pre-flight check-off. 423 Squadron RCAF, April 6th, 1943.

Above: PROP CHECK. Yet another item in the flight engineer's list to inspect and check. An excellent view of the let-down servicing platform which retracted into the wing's leading edge.

Left: SPARKS — the universal nickname for all members of the wireless trade, air and ground, and derived from the cloth badge worn on the sleeve (a 'fistful of lighting'), worn here by Sergeant L J Irving of 423 Squadron RCAF, August 1943.

43

all descriptions. The cooker was a nautical contraption called the Clyde Cooker — consisting of an oven in the middle of two Primus stoves in the outer sections providing two heating rings. After much practice we even managed to make reasonable cakes in the oven. Twenty five gallons of fresh water were carried in five drums with fitted taps, so a cup of tea or coffee presented no difficulty. Naturally we had a sink in which to carry out washing-up chores. We were equipped also with a handsome WC, flushed by an 11-gallon tank; our model was the 'Gosport Baby' and was a normal marine 'head'. In this small room was a wash basin and shaving mirror, so one could look spruce and clean before going ashore. An amusing (in retrospect) incident on my boat was an occasion when the toilet discharge system had a stoppage. I told the flight mechanic airframe to repair it, but he replied he had no spanner large enough for the job. Blocking the toilet door to prevent his escape, I told my other flight mech. to go ashore and fetch a large Stilson spanner. I stood in the doorway until the poor devil had completed his unpleasant but very necessary task, but still have a twinge of conscience about it until this day. Little incidents like this show the amount of hard work done by the crew in maintaining the boats in an airworthy and seaworthy condition. Apart from servicing of the engines, airframe and other systems, a lot of cleaning and polishing had to be done constantly. In addition, bilges had to be pumped daily — the Sunderland was equipped with a fitted bilge system, pumped out by an APU through a valve control.

During our hours aboard, after work was finished, we often indulged in slightly ridiculous pastimes. Mustard sandwiches for seagulls was one 'amusement'. while another was to tie two sandwiches together, whereupon two gulls would swallow individual sandwiches and an airborne battle would ensue until one was forced to disgorge. We furnished the wardroom with coloured curtains and a portable radio. Normally we had a couple of the crew aboard at night in case an emergency cropped up. During gale warnings this crew would be a pilot and the flight engineer. The aircraft would be fitted with storm pennants and if things became particularly rough the engines (usually the outers) would be started to take the strain off the buoy. Once, during a short stay at Poole, an armourer came out to my friend Joe Bellamy's Sunderland, ran out the bombs

to check circuits, and inadvertently jettisoned the lot. Joe became somewhat worried that the six depth charges might explode in spite of their safety clips being on; and therefore decided to move his boat. Without ever having taxied a boat before, he started his outer engines, cast off after some difficulty and managed to attach himself to another buoy. Unbeknown to him, our CO, Wg Cdr Lovelock, had watched these interesting manoeuvres from the shore — hands over his eyes! As he remarked to Joe subsequently, 'That's one of those things where, if you're successful, you get a pat on the back; but if you hit something you'd have been right in it. . .'

Mention must be made of the men who manned the marine craft. We Sunderland crews relied on them for everything whilst afloat — fuel, bombs, food and personal transport. They always seemed to get us aboard in the most appalling weather conditions without ever damaging the aircraft. On November 16th we flew an air/sea rescue attempt, but having located the dinghy we found the sea too rough to land, and therefore remained throughout the night dropping flares until we were relieved by another aircraft. This sortie completed our 300 hours, and by this time Australian flight engineers were arriving. Volunteers had been requested to form a new Coastal Command Halifax squadron and Joe Bellamy (who had never lost his love of Merlin engines) talked me into going with him. It was not the same, flying in any old aircraft that happened to be serviceable, and no happy life aboard servicing and polishing one's 'own' aircraft. The Sunderland is still, to me, the aircraft which I look back on with affection. I suppose it was a life akin to that of the crew of a well-found yacht, and we were quite self-sufficient, being able to live on board, service our own kite, and had an inexhaustible number of possible bases.

Left: CHAIN GANG. Sergeants Jack Shand and Bill Beale stow the mooring chain in its nose locker by means of the winch in foreground. The anchor can be seen to the left of the winch. 423 Squadron RCAF, April 6th, 1943.

Above left: TOP BRASS. Air Chief Marshal Sir Frederick Bowhill, KCB, CMG, DSO, who commanded RAF Coastal Command during the early years of the war. Known irreverently as 'Ginger' by all, his most recognisable feature — almost a trademark — was a pair of fierce, curling eyebrows . . .

Above: SCRAMBLED EGG OMELETTE. A gathering of Coastal Command's Group commanders at Coastal Headquarters, Northwood, Middlesex. From left: AVM G B A Baker CB, MC; Air Cmdre A H Primrose, CBE, DFC; AVM J M Robb, CB, DSO, DFC, AFC; AVM A Durston, AFC; Air Cdre S P Simpson, CBE, MC; ACM Sir Phillip Joubert, KCB, CMG, DSO, (who succeeded Sir Frederick Bowhill as AOC-in-C); AVM G R Bromet, CBE, DSO; Air Cdre I T Lloyd, CBE; and Air Cdre H G Smart, CBE, DFC, AFC.

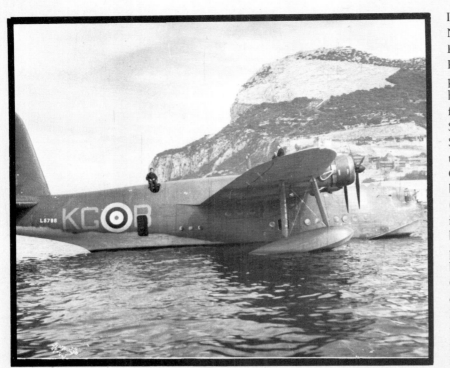

In May 1934, a young man started work in No. 3 Shop of the Short Brothers' Works at Rochester. He had been a student with Rollaston Aviation at Ford, Sussex for a couple of years before arriving at Rochester and his initial employment at Shorts, under foreman Harry Gregg, was on the Short Scion Junior aircraft. A later move onto Singapore III flying boats, and eventually into the drawing office, firmly established Ray Gough's loyalties both to Shorts and flying boats. In a new section of the drawing office (under the aegis of Bill Doughty) he became involved in work on the civil Empire flying boats and finally an exciting new military project, Specification R2/33 — later to become the Sunderland. The 1938 Munich Crisis saw Gough join (as a wireless operator/air gunner) No 500 (County of Kent) Squadron, AAF and he soon transferred to the RAF Volunteer Reserve for pilot training — the latter eventually beginning in June 1940. His one ambition was sim-

Novice to Captain

Ray Gough

Below: SIESTA. T9070, KG-E of 204 Squadron at moorings, basking in the tropical heat of Bathurst, early 1942. This aircraft joined 204 in December 1940 and continued to serve with the unit until August 16th, 1942, on which date it exploded while being rearmed.

ple — to fly flying boats. By virtue of hard work during training, he finally achieved a posting to the FB Training Squadron at Stranraer, Scotland, where his real introduction to the 'mysteries' of sea-going aviation commenced in Short Singapore IIIs and Saro Londons. Then, in May 1941, a sergeant-pilot, he was one of six embryo 'boat skippers freshly posted in to 204 Squadron, based at that time in Iceland.

Left: L5798, KG-B, 204 Squadron, moored in Gibraltar Bay, 1942. It had a varied career, making its first flight on September 1st, 1938, serving with 210 and 201 Squadrons, and joining 204 in July 1941. It remained with 204 until October 1st, 1943, when it was flown to Calshot.

ALL AIRMEN, WHEREVER YE MAY BE, GREETINGS: KNOW ALL YE BY THESE PRESENTS, THAT

F/Lt. G.A. POTTER

DID, ON 7th SEPT. '43 APPEAR IN THE NORTHERNMOST REACHES OF MY REALM, ENPLANED IN THE A/c MV120, IN LATITUDE 66°-33N, AND LONGITUDE 26° 32'W, BOUND FOR THE DARK AND FROSTY WASTES OF

THE LAND of the MIDNIGHT SUN

AND DID, WITH MY ROYAL PERMISSION, ENTER THIS DREAD REGION BY

☉ CROSSING THE ARCTIC CIRCLE ☉

BY VIRTUE WHEREOF, I, NEPTUNUS REX, RULER OF THE RAGING MAIN, DO HEREBY DECLARE HIM TO BE A LOYAL AND TRUSTY Bluenose, AND DO CALL UPON ALL ICEBERGS, SEALIONS, NARWHALS, POLAR BEARS, WHALES,

AND OTHER CREATURES of the FRIGID NORTH, TO SHOW HIM DUE DEFERENCE AND RESPECT. DISOBEY UNDER PAIN OF MY ROYAL DISPLEASURE!

Aurora Borealis
QUEEN OF HIS MAJESTIES NORTHERN PROVINCES

Neptunus Rex
RULER OF THE RAGING MAIN
BY HIS TRUSTY SERVANT

CERTIFICATE No 641

GROUP CAPTAIN RAF
PRIVATE SECRETARY

AIR COMMODORE. RAF.

'Our arrival, all non-regular (i.e. RAFVR) pilots was shock enough to the squadron, but three of us were sergeants and this was traumatic, especially to the other NCO tradesmen. However, with great goodwill on all sides, we were accepted into the 'Flying Boat Union' on our merits and were quickly allotted to crews — supernumary at first but sooner than we expected as full members. In those days one started as 2nd pilot and learned from both the 1st pilot and the skipper. In the fullness of time skippers were posted tour-expired, promoted to flight-commander, or in other ways made vacancies for the 1st pilots to become skippers, and 2nd pilots to become 1st pilots. There had been very occasional NCO — usually Warrant Officer — skippers, but only regular long-term serving airmen. (Of these, the 'Three W's' were famous (notorious?) throughout Coastal Command — Warrant Officers Williams, Walters and Wheeler. I came to know them all at various times, and great companions they were.) Normally the FB Union was very much an officers-only organisation, at least as far as pilots were concerned. The 2nd pilot was very much a general dogsbody,

'joed' for refuelling supervision, moving boats, and gale guard. One's first gale guard was a shattering experience. An engine fitter, rigger and wireless operator comprised one's crew — all 'old sweats' with hundreds of hours flying and a natural suspicion of a brand-new sergeant-pilot's ability to cope with the frightening responsibility of safeguarding 25 tons of flying boat lurching about on its mooring. Looking back, one can only feel proud to have had this type of crew who, once they realised a new boy was not too proud to learn, gently taught all they had learned, and became fiercely loyal in their discussions as to how 'their' new pilot was coping. It is undoubtedly true to say that these crew members had as much to do as the skipper in moulding any future ability and character of new pilots on the squadron. Again if one was lucky, and I was, the skipper soon had one taking turns in take-offs and landings and spells at the controls during patrols, apart from giving the navigator a break. All Coastal Command pilots were navigators in their own right — and had a certificate to prove it. In those days things moved quickly on an FB squadron. My third

48

Far left: BLUENOSE CHIT. An example of the 'Blue Nose Certificate' given to all airmen who served within the Arctic Circle; in this case being 'awarded' to a member of 120 Squadron, a non-Sunderland unit.

Left: ON THE STEP. L2158, KG-M of 204 Squadron on full power as it gets airborne from Bathurst, West Africa. This was the first production Sunderland I, seen here fitted with four 1010 hp Pegasus 22 engines, and carrying 'stickleback' ASV radar aerials along its fuselage top. L2158 was eventually lost at sea during a patrol on August 17th, 1942.

Below left: T9072, KG-F, 204 Squadron, undergoing routine maintenance at Bathurst, early 1942. It had previously served with 10 Squadron RAAF.

Below: HOME FROM HOME. SS *Manela*, the floating accommodation for many Sunderland crews throughout the war, in places ranging as far afield as Scotland, Iceland and West Africa. Seen here, in 1946, anchored off Singapore.

49

operational flight — and sixth in total — on the squadron was a search for German 'naval units' on May 25th, 1941. These were, of course, the *Bismark* and *Prinz Eugen* — and the aircraft relieving us soon spotted the *Bismark* — with the now well-known result. My logbook shows for June 1941 a total of 170 hours flying — only 10 of which were not operational. An entry for July 13th, 1941 records the squadron (204) as operating from Reykjavik, Iceland, and on July 15th from Gibraltar, from where anti-submarine cover was required for the first convoys to Malta. By late August the squadron was based at Bathurst, in Gambia, West Africa. Initially we lived aboard a P. & O. 'liner' SS *Manela* (as we had done in Iceland on a sister ship, SS *Dumona*). Local small craft were hired to act as a marine craft section until the arrival of our own RAF personnel and boats. Eventually a camp was built on the shore at Bathurst and we all moved ashore.

On September 29th, 1941, while still 1st pilot to Fg Off Ken Dart who was our skipper, we were detailed for a patrol to the north-west and on our way back to do a recce of Dakar — at that period occupied by the Vichy French — to check a reported fire in fuel storage installations near the harbour. We crossed the coast about 20 miles north of Dakar at zero altitude and flew down the main road. The battleship *Richelieu* and a cruiser were moored parallel and about 200 yards apart in the harbour. We flew over the town, just above the rooftops, and then even lower over the water across the harbour. By flying so low and between the two warships we made things somewhat difficult for them to fire at us. We got away with the information we required unmarked, 'jinking' our way out to the open sea. Then we spotted four fighters rapidly overtaking us — Curtiss Mohawks of the Vichy French Navy. Handing over the controls to Ken Dart (standard procedure being for skippers to have prime control in any impending action), we prepared our Sunderland (N9044, 'C') for battle, but were relieved to see another Sunderland (J/204) angling in to join the party. All four Mohawks made a concerted attack, their first fire putting our rear turret out of action. During the next ten minutes Ken Dart manoeuvred 'Charlie' skilfully all over the sky, but the fighters managed to wound three of our crew — I was hit through the wrist — while one bullet set off a flare inside our Sunderland and started a fire. The end of the immediate affair was that two Mohawks

were shot down (one each by us and Sunderland 'J') and the other pair flew home, damaged. We heard later that both of these crashed on landing and one pilot died days later. Our aircraft had a total of 74 bullet holes, a punctured fuel tank, u/s rear turret, and a fire up for'ard, apart from three wounded crew members. On arrival back at base we had to beach the Sunderland immediately or it would have sunk due to the bullet holes letting in water. Ken Dart was awarded a DFC for his handling of this affair, while I got a spell of home (sick) leave while my wrist mended. At a much later date, while instructing on Sunderlands at No 4(C) OTU, a delightful twist of fate brought this whole incident back to me. A number of French naval pilots were attending for flying boat conversion and one wore the ribbon of a *Croix de Guerre*. As we were going out to Sunderland N9044 for a spot of dual instruction, I asked this particular Frenchman for what he had been awarded his medal. He replied, 'For shooting down a Sunderland'. Further query as to the details brought the surprising answer that the 'victory' took place at Dakar — on September 29th, 1941! I must admit that it was with considerable relish that I then showed him over his 'victim', N9044, moored in the bay. The Frenchman, however, derived some satisfaction from counting the still-visible patches over the many bullet-holes in wings and hull.

On June 4th, 1942, I finally received the 'accolade' by being given captaincy of my own Sunderland, N9024, 'H'-for Hornet (so-named from the cartoon insignia painted over the entry hatch — a hornet sharpening its sting on a grindstone). Random extracts from my logbook give details of many diverse flights. For example, the search for a fellow-squadron Sunderland 'V' (Flt Lt Ennis) which crashed on patrol on June 28th, 1942. On July 1st, Hudson 'E' from our sister squadron, 200, at Bathurst, found the survivors in half-submerged dinghies and clinging to ropes, signalled their position to us and we stayed with the dinghies until the crew was rescued by HMS *Velox*. Watching one's friends being rescued after some 70 hours in the sea was a truly rewarding experience. Later in the same month, on July 24th, we were on another search for survivors, this time from the US m/v *Honolulan*, torpedoed the previous day by a U-boat. Co-operation between the Hudson and Sunderland squadrons resulted in three lifeboats being spotted. As skipper of a Sunderland, one con-

Right: HIGH AND DRY. T9072, KG-F, battened down and beached for major inspection servicing, Bathurst, West Africa.

Below: CLOSE COMPANION. KG-K of 204 Squadron, photographed during a patrol from Alness, 1943.

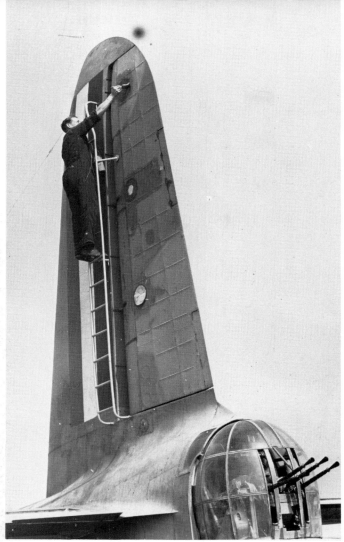

Left: TALE OF A TAIL. The sheer size of a Sunderland tail (in this case, DA-J of 210 Squadron) needed a head for heights by airframe tradesmen during routine maintenance. Here a rigger is repatching and doping worn sections of the rudder fabric.

Far left: ENGINE CHANGE. Two aspects of 228 Squadron's erks working on changing the port inner Pegasus of N9029, NM-V at Alexandria, Egypt, 1941.

Below: CALM WATERS. Outside check by riggers in the sunshine of West Africa.

Right: PRESSURE KILLER. Armourers crutch down a 450lb depth charge on the mobile bomb rack — a job needing a fine sense of balance when working from a bobbing bomb scow or utility pinnace.

Far right: IT HAPPENS TO THE BEST . . . Sunderland T9071 of 10 Squadron RAAF which skipper Vic Hodgkinson taxied into a merchant tanker (it was not his error, but the tanker captain's . .) at Alexandria on June 2nd, 1941. The aircraft suffered wing-tip damage only. In the second photo the crew are refuelling some 2,000 gallons of petrol by hand and can. T9071 later served as NM-M of 230 Squadron and was lost when shot down off the Libyan coast (See LIBYAN EPISODE).

Far left, Centre: OUT OF ITS ELEMENT. W6055, ZM-R of 201 Squadron beached in September 1942. This aircraft was later used by A Flight, 330 (Norge) Squadron.

Far left, bottom: ON ICE. ML742, NS-Q of 201 Squadron, ice-bound at Lough Erne, Northern Ireland during the great freeze-up of January 1945 — one of the very few occasions when a crew could literally walk away from their aircraft.

Below: DD843, 'E' of 461 Squadron RAAF undergoing engine checks on its starboard inner, 1944.

Left: ANCHOR AWAY — stowing the sea anchor in the under-nose compartment. In foreground can be seen the mooring winch.

Below left: WRITE-OFF. A26-6, one of six Sunderland IIIs operated by 40 Squadron RAAF in Australia towards the end of the war. This view shows just part of the extensive damage resulting from a collision by Flight Lieutenant Williams with the dolphin at the Townsville harbour entrance, 1944. The aircraft was soon written-off charge as unrepairable.

printed on a large notice board, and fitters' and riggers' names written alongside. At the beginning I went out with the experienced riggers to learn DI's. Depending on where the aircraft was moored on the estuary, we sometimes boarded small dinghies, or used large pinnaces from the jetty at Pembroke Dock and then transferred to the small dinghies taking the mechs to the aircraft. The weather controlled our work, but in the mornings the sea was usually calm and we were able to get aboard the machines. The trouble was that as we worked the wind would spring up, the sea get choppy and, despite much flashing on our Aldis lamp from the cockpit, the marine craft would not bring us off until the sea abated. This usually meant we missed lunch and, quite often, tea. Our flight

sergeant often had to issue late meal chits, but the cooks were a patient lot and usually found us something to eat no matter what the hour.

The DI on a Sunderland consisted of checking mooring ropes and bridle, that the front gun turret would move smoothly back and forwards, the boat hook was intact, and that there were no snags with the bomb aimer's window (which fitted into the hull when the aircraft was flying). The aircraft toilet was a flush type and the rigger's job included pumping sea water into its cistern — though this was usually left until last thing before vacating the aircraft for obvious reasons. . . Canvas drogues, used for steering the aircraft onto its moorings, were housed in metal containers in the galley amidships on the lower deck. A pilot would indicate which

PANORAMA. Part-view of the maintenance area of Castle Archdale station, Northern Ireland, on September 28th, 1944. These particular Sunderlands are from 422 Squadron RCAF.

Above: PARKING BAY.
Three of 422 Squadron
RCAF's Sunderland IIIs —
left is ML883, 'V' and right,
ML857 — outside their
hangars at Castle Archdale,
June 28th, 1944.

Far left: CHECK FOR
EASE OF MOVEMENT —
a sergeant engine fitter
carries out part of a routine
inspection of the skipper's
throttle levers. A 10
Squadron RAAF machine.

Left: PLUGS AND POTS.
Engine fitters sort out a
snag on the starboard inner
Pegasus of a 10 Squadron
RAAF Sunderland.

Right: DANGER —
WOMEN AT WORK.
WAAF engine flight
mechanics, supervised by
an NCO fitter, tackle a
starboard outer engine at
Mountbatten, 1943.

Right: PHOTO FIENDS. LACs F B Hickey, B B Charach and G W Mason installing an F24 camera in the rear compartment of a 422 Squadron RCAF Sunderland III, Castle Archdale, December 8th, 1944.

Below: A LA MODE. Typical protective clothing for a beaching 'party' demonstrated here by a WAAF of Coastal Command, 1944.

Right: 'TWO-SIX' — all available hands to the ropes as P9600, DQ-T of 228 Squadron is manhandled along the slip. Previously 'E' of 10 Squadron RAAF, this Sunderland served with 4(C) OTU in early 1943.

Above left: TAKE THE STRAIN. Light tractor about to shift EK583, '3-J' of 423 Squadron RCAF at Castle Archdale, July 17th 1944.

Above: ROLLING. W4004, Z-Zebra on its way to the hangar, a scene at Mount Batten. A view showing incidentally the common wear and tear on fuselage paintwork by constant water abrasion.

Centre left: ON REFLECTION . . . ZM-S of 201 Squadron, on its beaching gear, provides a peaceful scene.

Below left: ON THE TROLLEY. L5803 in dry dock at Pembroke Dock, just before the war. It later saw operational service with 230 and 228 Squadrons.

Right: HANGAR VIEW. Sunderland III, ML874, DG-U of 422 Squadron RCAF on the servicing apron at Pembroke Dock, December 8th, 1944.

Libyan Episode

The Sunderlands of 228 and 230 Squadrons were employed in many operational theatres in a seemingly endless variety of tasks. In particular their successes against U-Boats in the Mediterranean theatre, their daring evacuation of hundreds of troops first from Greece then Crete and later similarly diverse operations in India and Burma come readily to mind. Merely as one example of the unique adventures which came the way of 230 Squadron crews is the story of a New Zealander, Flight Lieutenant (later Air Marshal) S. W. R. Hughes during December 1941.

Based at Aboukir, Egypt, Hughes was captain of Sunderland T 9071 — 'M for Margaret which took off about 2 am on Dec 21st to carry much needed supplies to Malta. In addition to his own crew Hughes was taking another New Zealander and his Wellington crew back to their squadron in Malta. Pilot Officer G. H. Easton had had to crash land in North Africa about a week earlier following battle damage while bombing Benghazi.

The incredible story of that Sunderland flight and its aftermath is illustrated by photographs taken by Sergeant Robinson, the gunner of the Sunderland. (When Robinson had to take to the water and swim for his life he first calmly sealed his camera in a tin and later retrieved it on the shore.)

Unlike the sunny Mediterranean of tourist fame, the weather was stormy, cold and bleak. Following take off the Sunderland ploughed its way through inky darkness to the west, fairly low and about 25 miles off the coast of Cyrenaica. Shortly after first light the alarm klaxon sounded as two Messerschmidt 110 fighters were sighted passing above and a few miles ahead. They were nearly out of sight when first one and then the other banked steeply and turned. The fight was on. The Sunderland quickly descended to a couple of

Flight Lieutenant S W R Hughes, skipper of T9071, 'M' (centre) with Pilot Officer Tony Jillings (white overall) and (right) Sergeant Stewart, on the wing of the wreck as they 'sailed' it towards the reef.

Above: Hughes using the Aldis lamp to signal to shore before striking the reef.

Right: Sunderland T9071, M, breaking up against the rocky shore-line in foreground, Pilot Officer Jillings.

the rolling seas. The hull was not damaged and only one wing tip float had been wrenched off. The crew clambered smartly out on the port wing, rigging life lines as they went thus preventing the Sunderland from dipping its unsupported wing into the sea and capsizing. It was then a matter of practising the drill of 'sailing' the Sunderland stern first before the strong north easterly wind by use of the rudder and controls. After some hours of searching the sky for further fighters and pumping the Sunderland clear of water and petrol leaking through shell holes, the coast loomed near with heavy seas breaking on an outlying reef.

Soldiers could be seen on the shore and, assuming they were British, a message was flashed by lamp asking for assistance for the crew when they swam ashore. Using the drogues or sea anchors the Sunderland was manoeuvred broadside-on shortly before it struck the reef so that the damaged starboard wing would overlap the rocks and thus give the crew some chance of avoiding the waves as they crashed on to the rocks. The big seas now struck the underside of the wing sticking up to windward and a few frightening moments ensued when the huge flying boat was nearly rolled over across its full wing span of 110 feet. All 19 men clung desperately to the life line and only released themselves in pairs at the signal given by their captain

hundred feet above the sea so the fighters could not attack from underneath and the first German made a suicidal but highly effective attack coming into point blank range dead astern with his two cannon and four machine guns firing. All eight guns of the Sunderland were brought to bear upon him and he disappeared, probably destroyed. He had however done irreparable damage to both engines and the ailerons on the flying boats starboard wing.

The remaining Messerschmit carried out several attacks from the beam and in the process the two midship gunners were wounded. Suddenly the German broke off his attack and disappeared streaming black smoke. This relief came none too soon as Hughes was having great difficulty in keeping his heavily laden flying boat airborne with only two engines working on one side and no ailerons on the other. He managed to turn into wind and carried out an emergency landing in the rough seas below. The 'boat ricocheted off two big waves but came to a fully stalled final landing in a trough between

80

slightly in advance of a breaking wave. With their Mae Wests inflated they were thus picked up by the broken seas and carried swiftly into calmer water inshore.

Flt Lt Odhams was given morphia and put in a rubber dinghy in charge of Sgt Dupont, an Australian experienced in surf lifesaving, and both reached the shore safely. The second pilot, Flt Lt Squires, fell off the wing and to the horror of those watching was sucked down by the undertow and disappeared beneath the Sunderland only to reappear later drifting out to sea beyond the breakers. The crew having all left the Sunderland, Flt Lt Hughes then dived overboard and after a struggle lasting over half an hour managed to bring Squires to the shore.

Shortly after, the party apart from one of the Wellington crew who had been killed outright during the air battle, gathered together, all bitterly cold, on the jagged rocks beneath Cape Appolonia about 100 miles east of Benghazi. No one had been seen on the shore and no help appeared to be forthcoming. Suddenly a group of Italian infantrymen appeared around a bluff. No weapons had been salvaged so Hughes went forward unarmed to meet them. There was no command to surrender so Hughes held out his hand in greeting. The leading soldier put his rifle aside and the two shook hands. The Italians were friendly and helpful and soon had a big

fire going and were helping to revive some of the airmen who were suffering from exposure.

The British had not recovered from their surprise at their friendly reception when another party of Italians lead by a bumptious lieutenant arrived and declared the British to be his prisoner. Pretending not to understand any of his orders, the British took little notice of him and in this seemed to have the support of a lot of the Italians. Then a short stocky little major arrived with about 100 more soldiers. He was quickly christened 'Musso' and it was soon apparent he was the senior officer of the remnants of the 102nd Caribineri which in the face of a swift advance by the 8th Army had had their motor transport taken by their allies, the Germans, while they were left to escape as best they could on foot around the coast. They had neither rations nor water. They were not at all enthusiastic about the war; all they wanted to do was to return to their families in Italy.

Hughes, however, had other things on his mind at this time. On the plea that the seriously

Top: Setting up the life-line to help Flt Lt. Hughes and Flt. Lt. Squires to reach the shore. Fg. Off Murphy holds a cut head, Fg Off Jilling's overalls are torn. The rock were razor sharp.

Above: Less than two hours after hitting the reef, M-Mother's back is broken by the continuous pounding against the rocks.

Above: The wounded crew member Flt. Lt Odhams lies in one of the dinghies (left). Sergeant Dupont, RAAF, in the other dinghy took him through the surf and safely ashore. Tragically, Odhams died a few days later.

Right: Captives. The Italians take charge. The sergeant air gunner in the foreground, with wounded hand, was one of the 172 Wellington Squadron crew passengers — he received his wound during the Sunderland air combat. He is smoking a cigarette courteously provided by his captors.

wounded Odhams should have some warm footwear he persuaded the Italians to let him swim back to the wreck of the Sunderland which was fast breaking-up and bring back some flying boots. He secured the boots, but in addition he cut open the bottom of a canvas sack containing about 100lbs weight of gold sovereigns which he had been carrying to the headquarters in Malta. He emptied them all into deep water and so intent was he that the enemy should not obtain the gold, he neglected to put even one sovereign in his pocket.

A stretcher to carry Flt Lt Odhams was improvised from the oars of the dinghy and now semi-conscious Odhams was carried first by the British and then in turns by the Italians along the precipitous shore. It was hard going and only slow progress was made. It was generally believed that Italian soldiers were rewarded for capturing British airmen and that the routine was to get then to an airfield as quickly as possible for transhipment to Italy. Hughes and his party therefore decided to use every ploy to delay things as much as possible.

Storms of rain and hail were still sweeping in from the sea and periodically lightning illuminated the leaden sky; as night fell everyone was ordered to lie down as they were; no fires were permitted as the Italians were very nervous of the local Arabs and their indiscriminate sharp shooting. With no food and with the only water available coming from pools in the rock, it was far from comfortable. Flt Lt Odhams was delirious and visibly sinking and Squires was still suffering

from shock and exposure. The party huddled close together around their ailing comrades and took turn to massage them and keep their circulation flowing. The second day was another nightmare of growing fatigue and difficulty in carrying the stretcher. The Italians repeatedly refused to carry it and insisted that the wounded man and one escort be left behind. The British however sat down and refused all orders to move unless their wounded comrade was also brought along. The Italians, sympathetic and kindly by nature, yielded to pressure.

Late in the afternoon Flt Lt Odhams died. The Italians wanted to cover his body with the usual cairn of rocks but the British insisted that a proper grave be dug in spite of the difficulty of doing this in the rocky ground. Again the Italians agreed reluctantly, but the work took some hours and captors and captives joined together in a short sad burial service. As Hughes repeatedly reminded his men 'things would be very different if we were prisoners of the Germans!'

Earlier in the day Hughes had accused the Italian major of commanding a rabble, unworthy of its reputation as one of Italy's proudest regiments, for someone had stolen Odham's flying boots while his stretcher was being rested. Immediately all the soldiers were formed into a line and searched. The boots were located and the culprit was pinioned by two of his companions while the major personally laid into him with a cat 'o nine tails which he carried like a bandolier. Hughes quickly intervened and said that honour had been more than satisfied.

In the middle of the cold uncomfortable second night the British suddenly realised they had visitors. Two Senussi Arabs had stealthily made their way past the sentries and claimed that they could get word to the 'Breetish'. A couple of notes were hurriedly scribbled on the pages of a pocket diary giving the identity and number of the prisoners and their captors, their position, mean line of advance and a plea for assistance. Both notes it turned out were delivered promptly into the British lines and a mortar section of the 4th Indian Division was sent to the rescue. This information, however, was not revealed until later.

Meanwhile the British had been telling the Italians constantly that their route of escape had been cut off by the 8th Army and by various ruses had convinced that this was so. At dawn the next day the major declared that forced marches were imperative and Hughes played his last card. One of his crew who had

Above: The long walk. Italians and RAF crews during the trek towards the Allied lines.

Above right: End of the trail. A group photo of the survivors, plus some local native gentry, after reaching Tmimi.

Far right: Sergeant Robinson, an air gunner and rigger of the Sunderland crew, who took all the remarkable photos of this adventure.

badly blistered feet as a result of playing tennis barefoot had his feet suitably 'doctored' so that they looked a terrible and bloody mess. Hughes declared that this man had to be carried by stretcher with all that was implied. The major was horrified at the prospect and was immediately given an alternative. The British were perfectly prepared to be left behind as a complete party and take their chance of survival at the hands of the Arabs. In addition they would furnish the major with a note addressed to any Allied Commander saying that he had treated his prisoners with exceptional fairness and therefore if he should be taken prisoner similar consideration should be given to him and his men. After a laborious translation of the document written on Italian foolscap, the major accepted and he and his men departed. Before going he even considered seriously a request to leave a couple of rifles and ammunition but on second thoughts felt that this was contrary to strict military protocol!

The Italians were no sooner gone than the Arabs appeared. A brisk trade ensued in which one wrist-watch procured two eggs, and one Egyptian pound a small bag of dates and some thick sweet coffee. For the promise of more 'felouse' to be paid on safe arrival in the British lines, a donkey was provided to carry the sick and the Arabs also supplied a couple of guides. Soon a strange column of 17 RAF aircrew and one British Army Major, a close friend of Hughes who had undertaken the flight for 'air experience', and their Senussi guides marched off south across the escarpment toward the British lines — the man with the blistered feet setting a smart pace!

Scattered groups of Italian soldiers were sighted and carefully avoided but soon the party blundered into a clearing where a number of exhausted Italians were resting. They were friendly but careless about their weapons and when the RAF party continued on, unmolested, they were in possession of a

84

was only too accurate. The nose gunner, Sergeant H. E. Finn, and the 2nd pilot, Flying Officer D M Wettlaufer, were wounded; while a shell from the sub's 4·7inch gun smashed against the Sunderland's fuselage, almost knocking it off track. Bishop kept the aircraft steady, however, and, running over the submarine from astern, released a stick of six depth charges. As these fell away the full effect of the flak on the Sunderland reduced it to a flying write-off. With aileron controls shot away, hull punctured in dozens of places and fires raging in the bomb room, galley and port wing, Bishop saw no alternative but to ditch quickly. Warning his crew, he set the stricken Sunderland down on the sea. '. . .we bounced once, twice, three times on the swell, the the port wing dropped. Its float was

Above: AUSSIE KILL. U-26 after a second attack run by Flight Lieutenant W N 'Hoot' Gibson of 10 Squadron RAAF in Sunderland 'H', July 1st, 1940. In foreground is the aftermath of a depth charge explosion near-miss. Within minutes the U-Boat commander scuttled his ship.

Far left & above:
COMBINED KILL. U-106
before and during a
combined attack made by
Flight Lieutenant Irwin
'Chick' Clarke (M/461
Squadron RAAF) and
Flight Lieutenant R D
Hanbury (JM708, N/228
Squadron) on August 2nd,
1943. The submarine
exploded and sank
vertically.

Centre left: GOING DOWN
. . . an anti-sub bomb leaves
a Sunderland bomb rack at
50 feet.

Below left: FOUR IN 10
DAYS. One of the for U-
Boats sunk by Sunderlands
during early August 1943.

torn off, the wing-tip immediately dug in and the kite cartwheeled into the sea. One second there was an almighty crash and the next we were in the water. The port wing had disappeared and a fire blazed where it should have been. The starboard wing, also on fire by then, and the fuselage were still afloat. One of the boys sat on the tailplane for a while but soon had to swim for it as the Sunderland went down within five minutes of ditching.'

After leaving the wreckage Bishop swam across to the wounded Finn (a non-swimmer) and supported him until help arrived from another crew member; while Flying Officer Mountford gave similar aid to the wounded Wettlaufer. Looking around the immediate area Bishop could see only five other men from his original 11-man crew. In the event four of the missing men were never seen again, while the body of the fifth was later recovered from the water and subsequently buried at sea. After nearly half an hour in the sea the crew saw their recent opponent, the U-boat, approaching them with a distinct stern-down list. It stopped about 200 yards from the airmen who watched the Germans abandoning their ship, taking to rafts. Soon both crews were floating in the water, watching the death throes of the submarine which sank slowly, its bow rising higher and higher towards the sky. There was a shattering explosion, followed quickly by two underwater blasts—and the U-boat was gone. The U-489 had made its last dive. For the next hour the six airmen and 58 surviving Germans floated less than 100 yards apart, neither group attempting to communicate with the other, in an uneasy enforced 'armistice'. Then rescue in the shape of a whaler from the RN destroyer *Castleton* arrived and took aboard both parties. Steaming at top speed to Iceland, the *Castleton* eventually offloaded the survivors and the wounded airmen were speedily transferred to hospital. The Sunderland skipper, Bishop was awarded an immediate DFC for 'gallantry and determination of a high order'.

In the afternoon of March 10th, 1944, Flight Lieutenant Sid Butler (RAF), one of the original members of 422 ('Flying Yachtsmen) Squadron RCAF, took off in Sunderland U-Uncle from Castle Archdale to carry out a routine search mission over the Atlantic west of Ireland. The trip was dual-purpose in that Butler was also supervising (in official terminology, screening) Warrant Officer W. F. Morton for whom this was his

Far left: SPOT-ON. U-243, a 500-tonner, gets a direct hit from Flying Officer W B Tilley, skipper of Sunderland H/10 Squadron RAAF, 130 miles south-west of Brest on July 8th, 1944. In foreground can be seen the machine gun fire tracks, which killed the captain and coxswain of the U-Boat.

Far left, bottom: ITALIAN VICTIM. Ferocious water plumes denote a perfect straddle on an Italian submarine in the Mediterranean, 1943.

Above: U-Boats were by no means the only marine targets for Sunderlands. Here an enemy merchant tanker receives a pair of bombs across its bows.

Centre left: NIGHT LIGHTS. A U-Boat revealed dramatically in the light of flares dropped by Flight Lieutennt L H Baveystock, DFM of 201 Squadron skippering DD829, 'Z' in the early hours of June 7th, 1944. Later that day, flying ML760, 'S', Baveystock sank the U-955; and on August 18, 1944, at the controls of EJ150, 'W' also sank U-107. He was awarded a DSO6 and 6DFC.

Below left: DEATH THROE. U-426 sinking by the stern on January 8th, 1944, after a depth charge attack by Flying Officer J P Roberts in Sunderland U-Uncle of 10 Squadron RAAF. Centre right can be seen one UB crew member blasted off the conning tower by the Sunderland gunners' fire during the run-in.

95

first operational patrol as a flying boat skipper. The outward leg was uneventful until, when 400 miles out over the grey ocean, flying at 1,000 feet, Butler spotted a submarine surfaced about six miles away on his port beam. He judged its speed at 12-15 knots — a sitting duck *if* he could reach it before it submerged. Shouting his crew to action stations, Butler rammed open the throttles and headed straight for the sub. Almost in the same moment the German crew commenced long-range fire from its conning tower guns and began a series of zig-zag manoeuvres to put off the Sunderland's aim. As the Sunderland came nearer, the submarine swung its stern towards the aircraft. At first Butler attempted a bow-on attack but the sub's expert manoeuvring and the hail of defensive flak baffled this approach. Ignoring the flak, Butler then slid into a beam attack from the starboard side of the U-boat and released a perfect straddle of depth charges slap across the sub's conning tower; while his gunners seized the opportunity to rake the body of the submarine as it came into range. As the aircraft roared over its target flak tore a series of jagged holes in its hull and Butler heaved the Sunderland into a steep bank and cleared the danger zone quickly. At the same moment the Sunderland's crew saw the eruption of their depth charges exactly on target but were then dismayed to see the U-boat begin to emerge from the fountain of boiling spray. It was only a matter of seconds however before the submarine, trailing a heavy oil slick, began circling slowly to starboard. With all his depth charges gone Butler could only watch and pray and for the following hour and a half the Sunderland circled the crippled U-boat, waiting. Then, to the astonishment of the aircraft crew, a message was flashed up to them 'Fine bombish' (sic), and they next saw about 40 members of the German crew begin to abandon ship, taking to rubber dinghies and pulling away from the now sinking submarine. As the sub gradually sank stern-first, the survivors, obviously well disciplined in dinghy drill, clustered the frail dinghies together in mutual support. The jubilant Sunderland crew continued to circle the dinghies for a further hour until finally relieved by another squadron Sunderland, skippered by Squadron Leader Grant. Sid Butler then set course for base. On the return leg the crew plugged all flak holes in the Sunderland's hull with rags and even chewing gum; these hasty 'repairs' proving sufficiently seaworthy to allow

Butler to land at base without further trouble. A well-earned DFC award was later made to Butler, not only in recognition of his destruction of U-625, but also of his sterling work during an extended tour of operations with 422 Squadron.

Although the hunting and killing of U-boats was a primary objective for Sunderland crews, one constant duty which was always paramount was that of convoy protection. With its long range and endurance the Sunderland usually combined the two by meeting merchant shipping convoys in mid-ocean and escorting them to safer waters. In the process they maintained a watch and ward for any would-be attackers and, when opportunity presented itself, were swift to destroy or, at least, nullify any threat to the helpless vessels in their charge. An example of this 'dual' role took place on October 8th, 1943, when Wing Commander J. R. Frizzle, on temporary attachment to 423 Squadron RCAF prior to his appointment to command its sister unit, 422 Squadron, had rendezvoused with his convoy and was two hours flying into the return leg of his patrol:

'I was flying with the crew of J-Jig as escort to convoy SC 143, and we were carrying out a 'Frog' patrol as ordered by the SNO (Senior Naval Officer). I was piloting. For

Far left: DAMAGED. Two views of U-71 under intensive attack by Flight Lieutenant S R C Wood in U-Uncle, 10 Squadron RAAF on June 5th, 1942. U-71, though seriously damaged, managed to limp back to La Pallice for repairs.

Four stages in the destruction of U-625 by Flight Lieutenant S W Butler in Sunderland 'U' of 422 Squadron RCAF on March 10th, 1944. Below: The first pair of depth charges explode around the UB's stern, while the rear AG's fire splashes the conning tower.

Inset above: Seconds later, the full force of the underwater explosion sends a chunk of the sub's structure hurtling through the air.

This page: As the U-Boat sinks stern-first, its crew scramble overboard and swim for the various dinghies floating nearby.

Above right: U-Boat survivors cluster their dinghies together for mutual aid. They are alone on the sea — 400 miles west of Ireland.

several hours the weather had been very poor, there being much cloud and continuous light and heavy rain. At our height (500 feet) we could see the water about 50 per cent of the time, visibility varying from zero to a mile. Flying had to be done mostly on instruments and as pilot I was unable to act as lookout to any great degree. As we came out of a cloud I noticed the 2nd pilot, Flying Officer A Menaul, lean forward for a better look at something. I looked too and saw a prominent wake ahead, its source being hidden from my view by the nose of the aircraft. The wake was scarcely 200 yards away and almost immediately Menaul yelled, 'It's a submarine'. There was a very strong wind and in a matter of seconds we had drifted to starboard enough for me to identify the conning tower of a fully-surfaced U-boat. I continued on approximately the same course until far enough past the sub to allow for a good attacking run. Then I began to turn to port and told Menaul to get the captain (Flying Officer A H Russell) to take over. In the meantime the skipper had instructed the wireless op to send out a '465' (Sighting Report) and had ordered the depth charges to be rolled out. When Russell took over we were 500 feet above the water and not more than 700 yards from the sub. I stood between

the two pilots to watch as Russell partially closed the throttles and dived at a fairly steep angle because of our proximity to the target. The U-boat had opened fire as we turned, but the shots were wild and well below us. On the other hand our nose gunner's 50's were ricochetting off the hull and conning tower in all directions and before the range had been reduced to 200 yards, the enemy's 4·7inch gun was silenced. We passed over the sub at 100 feet, and as we climbed to port, the galley look-out advised that three depth charges had dropped and a fourth failed to release. Numbers 1 and 2 had fallen to port, and No 3 to starboard abreast of the conning tower, which lifted 15 to 20 feet as No 2 depth charge exploded. We turned in for a second attack but there was no longer a submarine. Instead, there were 15 or more Germans, surrounded by debris, swimming about in a rapidly spreading patch of oil. My instantaneous impression was that the U-boat had been definitely destroyed. The remaining depth charges were rolled back into the fuselage.' Sunderland J-Jig, by then 33 minutes beyond official recall time, was headed for home, there to report the death of *Unterseeboot* U-610; and three months later the skipper, A H Russell, was awarded a Distinguished Flying Cross.

99

Greater Love has no man

By October 1943 the U-boat 'Wolf-Pack' tactics reached their peak, without the hoped-for successes envisaged by their originator, Admiral Karl Dönitz. In the same month a general order was issued to U-boat commanders to be prepared to defend themselves from air attack by fighting on the sea surface instead of adopting the more natural ploy of crash-diving to anonymous safety in the depths of the ocean. German submarines had progressively been more heavily armed with 20mm and 37mm cannons mounted around and on conning towers and adjacent decks for just this purpose. The overall result was a steep increase in the dangers facing any attacking aircraft. However well a flying boat skipper might evade flak opposition during an attack approach the very nature of his

weapon system and target required him to fly directly over the submarine eventually, and the last few hundred yards of that bomb-run had to be rock-steady without evasion. U-boat captains were well aware of this and, with their formidable defences, were fully confident in their ability to take on all comers. They forgot one completely unpredictable facet — human determination no matter what the odds against final survival.

'Devotion to duty', 'aggressive spirit', 'courage and fortitude' — all these and varieties on the same theme were featured time and again in award citations to Sunderland captains throughout the war. And undoubtedly all were part of the 'determination' expressed in action by these men. But combined with such characteristics was

the universal responsibility felt by all aircraft captains to their aircraft and especially to their crews. Numerous examples exist of individual aircraft skippers who gave their lives ensuring, or attempting to ensure, the survival of their crew members. In the context of the Sunderland's war, just two examples might well illustrate this theme.

Flight Lieutenant Paul Sargent, an experienced skipper of 422 Squadron RCAF, set out in Sunderland S-Sugar on October 17th, 1943 for a convoy protection sortie over the mid-Atlantic area. His ten-man crew were all experienced men, with no illusions about the task ahead. Only one was not a regular member of Sargent's usual crew, Flight Lieutenant P A S Woodwark, the Group Gunnery Officer, who had 'come along for the ride' and was occupying the front gunner's turret for this sortie. Well out into the Atlantic Sargent made visual contact with his 'flock' of merchant ships and began the normal sweep of the adjacent sea, hunting for any possible threats. Almost immediately he spotted two U-boats, fully surfaced, and heading towards the convoy from some five miles distance. Without hesitation Sargent swung his Sunderland into an attack approach. Both submarines remained surfaced and opened up a devastating barrage of con-centrated flak. Selecting one U-boat as his intended victim, Sargent ordered Woodwark to fire on the German crew as the flying boat drew nearer, and the front guns momentarily cleared the submarine's deck. Releasing a stick of depth charges, Sargent banked away steeply, turning for a second run, and then realised that his first attack had undershot narrowly. To quote the 2nd pilot, Flying Officer Art Bellis, 'This time no evasive action was taken; only two depth charges were left and the skipper apparently determined that this attack had to be successful.'

As the Sunderland roared in for its second attack, it received the full fury of the combined flak from both submarines. Cannon shells ripped through the soft-skinned hull, killed Woodwark and another front gunner,

The seeming-pause seconds before a Sunderland alights; the moment when all the skill of the skipper is needed to set 25 tons of flying boat safely onto water. Sunderland III, EK591 about to land at Castle Archdale, July 15th, 1944.

Flight Sergeant L T Needham, tore the left leg off the navigator, Flying Officer C B Steeves, smashed the automatic pilot, R/T and W/T systems, destroyed the throttles and pitch exactors, tore out a wing dinghy, and ripped a hundred jagged holes in the forward fuselage skin. Paul Sargent refused to waver from his run and released his remaining pair of depth charges in a perfect straddle of the U-Boat's slim hull. (The rear gunner reported a perfect hit and saw the submarine lift bodily out of the water before it disappeared into the depths). As the shattered flying boat cleared the scene Steeves, the mortally wounded navigator, still incredibly standing at his station, gave the skipper the DR position and a course to steer for the nearest shipping. He then collapsed and died.

Sargent headed for the convoy and after briefly circling one of the escort ships, prepared to set the near-unmanageable Sunderland down as close as possible to the ship. Touching down in rolling waves, the aircraft bounced once and disintegrated. The tail assembly tore away and the remains of the aircraft plunged deep into the sea. Flight Sergeants J Y Rutherford and D Mesney, the former suffering from concussion and lacerations and the latter having a fractured leg and one paralyzed arm, managed to leave the wreckage through the open fuselage stern section. Art Bellis, wounded, unconscious and tangled in the radio aerials, owed his life to a seaman from the rescue frigate who swam to

SEA OF TROUBLES. A photo epitomising the lonely vigil over the trackless oceans that consituted the vast bulk of Sunderland crews' operational experiences throughout the war. RB-A of 10 Squadron RAAF on a solitary patrol 1940.

further combat and all headed for Norway. Aboard the Sunderland, Phillips took stock of his crew and aircraft. He had suffered a slashed eye-lid from flying splinters, while Armitstead and Godwin, the navigator, had also been cut by metal splinters. The damage to the aircraft was far worse. All fuel tanks were punctured and leaking, trimming gear wrecked, instrument panel damaged, and the hull, tail assembly and one bomb rack were all bullet-riven. Setting course for Invergordon, Phillips spent the next two hours struggling to maintain height, but finally made it and brought the Sunderland in for a safe landing. It was later confirmed that the

second Junkers hit had crash-landed in Norway and then been burned by its crew. Phillips was subsequently awarded a DFC, while Corporal Lillie received a well-earned DFM for his coolness under fire — the first time a Sunderland had engaged in air-to-air combat and achieved a victory.

Three years after Phillips' combat, the Sunderland's fighting capacity was again exemplified in an epic fight against frightening odds. Flight Lieutenant C B Walker of 461 (RAAF) Squadron was skipper of Sunderland N-Nan on June 2nd, 1943, engaged in an anti-submarine recce in the 'Derange' area, just west of the Bay of Biscay, when at 7 pm,

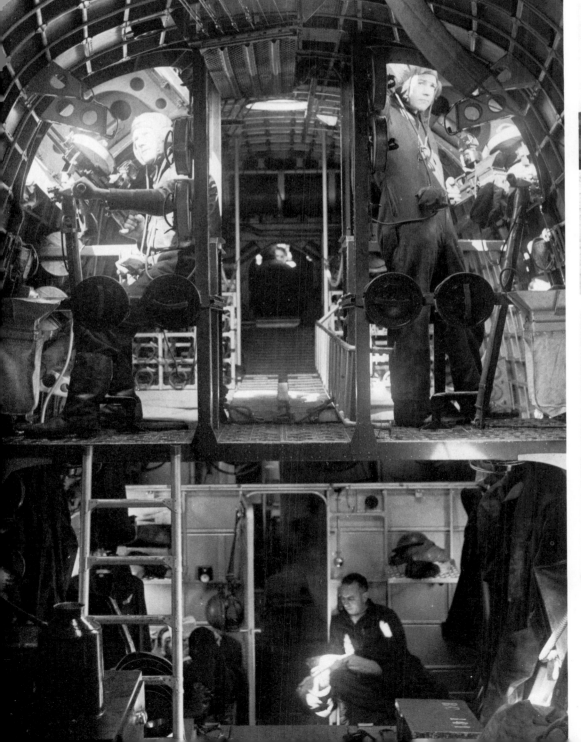

his tail gunner, Warrant Officer R M Goode reported a formation of eight Junkers 88's some six miles away and closing. The navigator, Flying Officer K M Simpson, immediately took up position in the astro-dome to act as fire controller, while all available crew members manned their guns, including the special galley hatch mountings devised on the squadron as extra defensive armament. Walker realised that an air combat was inevitable, promptly jettisoned all depth charges, had an enemy report signalled to base, and prepared for combat. The Junkers, obviously well drilled, split into small attack groups, three to port, three to starboard and two single aircraft hovering on the beams. Once disposed, the leading Junkers on both beams wheeled into attack. On the port side a burst of cannon shells ripped into the Sunderland's port outer engine which broke into flames; while other shells slashed across Walker's instrument panel, shattering the compass and spilling burning alcohol over both Walker and his 1st pilot, Pilot Officer W J Dowling. Punching the extinguisher button, Walker put out the fire in the engine, but the power plant was now useless. At the same time the skipper wrenched his lumbering aircraft into a series of violent evasive manoeuvres, twisting from side to side as each Junkers bore in. As the second wave attacked cannon shells ripped into the rear turret's hydraulics, knocking Goode unconscious, wounded Simpson and completely wrecked the radio and R/T system. Successive attacks — at least 20 such assaults were made — wreaked havoc throughout the Sunderland and its crew. A galley hatch gunner was mortally wounded, the body of the aircraft torn time and time again by cannon shell and bullet fire. But in the third onslaught, the midships gunner hammered a burst into one

Top: NOSE BARB. A Mk I Sunderland's forward defence, comprising here twin .303 VGO machine guns.

Above: Rear view — the FN13 tail turret with its four .303 Brownings, each fitted with flash eliminators at the muzzle.

Ju 88 which then received a full burst from the front guns and with cockpit shattered and an engine spewing flames, fell into the ocean below. A second Junkers, breaking away from its attack, took a full burst in its belly and spun down to crash. The battle raged on, with Walker and Dowling taking such violent evasive action that the hull became strained and all doors jammed. The wounded rear gunner, Goode, recovered consciousness and, due to the complete loss of his turret's hydraulics, operated the guns by hand. Combining with another gunner, he sent a third Junkers flaming into the sea. Finally, after nearly an hour of non-stop fighting, the remaining Junkers drew off, circled and gave up the struggle. Three of their original eight aircraft were burning in the water, while at least two others were seriously damaged.

For Walker it was not the end of the affair. He was 300 miles from base, in enemy territorial waters, flying a severely damaged aircraft with only three functional engines, no radio, a dead man on the lower deck, and virtually every crew member wounded to some degree. His own burns from the com-

pass alcohol were painful enough, but when added to the sheer physical exhaustion of flinging a Sunderland about like a Spitfire for 45 minutes, had almost rendered him powerless. Undeterred, Walker set course for base while the crew jettisoned everything loose to lighten ship. Hoping to make Pembroke Dock, Walker eventually made a landfall on the tip of Cornwall when another engine began to fail. With little alternative, and despite a hull riddled with shell holes, he set the aircraft down at Praa Sands, near Penzance, and as the flying boat settled the sea began to fill the shattered hull. In one final act of near-desperation the skipper gave his remaining engines full power and literally beached the Sunderland on the sandy shore, clear of the tide line. Subsequently Walker was awarded a DSO, the wounded Simpson received a DFC, while the rear gunner, Goode, was awarded a DFM. Tragically, three members of this crew — Dowling, Simpson and Goode — were lost only weeks later when, on August 18th, flying with another skipper, their Sunderland failed to return.

On November 19th, 1943, Flight Lieutenant Finucane and crew, of 228 Squadron, were engaged on an anti-sub patrol when four Junkers 88s were seen approaching some eight miles away on the starboard bow. The only cloud cover was a cumulus cloud some distance away and the Sunderland headed for this immediately. The Ju 88s attacked from the port quarter just as the Sunderland skipper jettisoned all his depth charges. Turning quickly, Finucane dived his aircraft underneath the Junkers and managed to enter cloud cover. Four times the Sunderland began icing up and was forced to leave the cloud and on at least nine occasions the attendant Junkers made single attacks, forcing the flying boat to evade violently and regain cloud shelter. Eventually the Sunderland was trapped in the open and two Junkers commenced a port bow climbing attack; while the others bore in from both port and starboard beams. The port galley gunner registered hits on one Junkers which promptly quit the scene and headed for France; but the climbing pair hammered bursts into the mid-fuselage. The three remaining Ju 88s then formed up, climbed to starboard, turned towards their target simultaneously and all three opened fire in a broadside assault. The Sunderland skidded to port, then turn to starboard in a tight diving turn. One Ju 88 attacking ahead was hit by the mid-upper gunner and flicked sideways pouring flames from its port engine. A second Junkers pressed its attack so close that it almost collided with the flying boat; while the third 88 roared over the top of the Sunderland only 15 feet away, offering a perfect belly shot to the Sunderland's rear gunner. It then broke off combat and headed towards France. The two remaining Junkers soon followed — the whole combat had lasted about 45 minutes. The Sunderland's only damage, apart from various shell holes in the fuselage, was to the aileron control chain which had jumped its sprocket during the many tight evasion manoeuvres. To balance, the gunners claimed one probable, and two damaged Junkers.

Eleven days later, on December 1st, another 228 Squadron Sunderland, skippered by Flight Lieutenant Grimshaw, was patrolling over the Bay of Biscay when he sighted eight Ju 88's four to five miles away. The subsequent combat was described later in *The Coastal Command Review* as follows: 'They were stepped up in line astern and flying a course at right angles to the Sunderland. The nearest one was slightly higher than the Sunderland. The formation at once headed for the flying boat, the leading Junkers peeling off and attacking on the starboard bow, coming in very close before breaking away. While fixing his gun in position the 2nd pilot was hit in the arm and forced to retire but the mid-upper and rear gunners got in several bursts at the Ju and tracers were seen to enter the aircraft. At this point the Sunderland was put into a violent diving turn to starboard, which caused the belt feeds in the tail turret to jump off their rollers, putting the four rear guns temporarily out of action . . . Two depth charges were jettisoned but the others hung up when the trolley jammed the bomb doors. The enemy aircraft which had been hit was last seen, by the tail gunner, diving vertically at the water, black smoke pouring from both engines. This appeared to disconcert the other Ju's and the second one made only a half-hearted effort, breaking off his attack at 1,000 yards. The rest of the formation wheeled to starboard and reformed. . . the whole lot flying parallel to the Sunderland. One aircraft made a dummy attack, breaking away at 800 yards; at the same time two Ju's attacked from the starboard bow but seemed reluctant to get in close and broke away at 1,000 yards, most of their fire bursting short. The Sunderland had not been drawn by the dummy attack and turned to meet this latter attack from the bow. Two other Ju's meanwhile came in at the port bow

and attacked in quick succession, firing from 2,000 yards to 800 yards. The first came in close after ceasing fire and was fired at by the front gunner. The Sunderland dived steeply to port and as the Ju passed above it was hit in the port engine by fire from the nose and mid-upper turrets. The tail gunner who had by then repaired his guns was able to get in a few short bursts as the enemy broke away. This Ju was seen to dive steeply towards the sea with black smoke coming from its port engine; and soon after a patch of foam was seen on the water. By this time the enemy formation was widely scattered and before it could regain formation the Sunderland was able to gain cloud cover. For about five minutes the crew caught glimpses of the enemy but no further contact was made. Continuing to circle in cloud for an hour, the Sunderland then set course for base. The action had lasted half an hour, and it was disappointing for the Sunderland gunners that the two Junkers which were almost certainly destroyed were not seen to crash and can therefore only be claimed as probables.'

A view of the improved tail defence, fitted in Sunderland EK590.

Mercy Angel

In addition to the many individual cases of Sunderlands rescuing survivors of torpedoed merchant shipping, ditched aircraft and other victims of the global maritime war, there were several outstanding occasions when, under fraught conditions, often under the very noses of a strong enemy force, the Sunderland became a vehicle of mercy. On each such occasion the highly individual prowess and initiative so characteristic of all flying boat crews was tested to the full; while the sheer versatility of the Sunderland was exemplified. In the early spring of 1941 British forces were assisting the magnificent defence of Greece against the Italian invaders, albeit with

pitifully few resources. Then at the start of April Hitler despatched a strong combination of air and land formations to bolster the unsuccessful efforts of his Axis partner and from that point on the Allied defence resolved into a bitter fighting retreat. First from the Greek homeland and eventually from Crete, there came a ragged flow of Allied servicemen, battered, exhausted but still determined to continue the fight. It was vital to the Allied cause that every man who could be retrieved from the advancing Axis assault be rescued. Normal air transport facilities were minimal — the RAF had yet to fully appreciate the overall importance of such a role — but im-

mediately available there was a handful of Sunderlands belonging to just two squadrons. 230 Squadron then based at Alexandria, Egypt, had been in the Mediterranean theatre of operations since May 1940; and 228 Squadron had joined them at Alexandria, arriving there in March 1941 via Malta (where one Sunderland, L2164, had been destroyed by an enemy fighter strafe on Kalafrana base on March 10th.) By April 16th, following the collapse of Yugoslavia and the consequent increase in German armed strength available to concentrate on the Greek assault, withdrawal of the Allied troops in Greece became of paramount importance. On that date 230 Squadron sent two Sunderlands to Kotor, Yugoslavia to evacuate 48 VIPs, including members of the royal family. Four days later Sunderland Y/230 began evacuation of RAF personnel from Greece, picking up a variety of passengers, essential freight and ammunition during a series of single sorties. In each case the Sunderland skipper was left very much to his own initiative. At first specific rendezvous points were given prior to take-off but there were many examples of Sunderlands dropping in ad hoc to likely evacuation points — and especially noteworthy were the many overload take-offs accomplished by the flying boat skippers. On April 23rd, 228 Squadron joined the 'Sunderland Taxi Service' when Flight Lieutenant Alex Frame lifted 50 RAF men from a Greek harbour and flew them to Suda Bay, Crete. On the same day two other Sunderlands, joined by a 'Converted' C-Class civil flying boat, between them evacuated a further 147 men to Suda Bay or Alexandria. One of these aircraft, Sunderland P/230 was later dive-bombed in Suda Bay and gutted by fire. Next day Alex Frame was ordered to fly to Nauplia Bay in the Bay of Argos to evacuate RAF men thought to be in that area. On arrival, just before dusk, however, he was told the RAF personnel had moved on, and he therefore took aboard 25 other men, including a general. Frame decided to wait for daylight before attempting to take-off in unknown waters but at dawn he found the whole bay enveloped in dense smoke from a burning ammunition ship and a bombed-out troopship. Taxying around for a while hoping for a clear take-off path, Frame finally made a blind take-off through the smoke. His

MOON MINION. N9029, NM-V of 228 Squadron gets airborne at dusk from Alexandria, Egypt, early 1941. It was to play a large part in the evacuation of Allied personnel from Greece and Crete during the early summer of that year.

Below: SWANS ASWIMMING. Two of 228 Squadron's Sunderlands temporarily moored off the Greek coast, early 1941, awaiting a load of Service evacuees. Centre is NM-X.

Above left: N9029, NM-V of 228 Squadron patrolling in the eastern Mediterranean, early 1941. It had previously served with 10 Squadron RAAF.

Above right: PIONEER. L5802, formerly 'E' then RF-F of 204 Squadron in which Flight Lieutenant (later Wing Commander) John Barrett won a DFC for his part in rescuing the crew of the torpedoed SS *Kensington Court* on September 18th, 1939. A veteran aircraft, it later served as SE-F with 95 Squadron, and then U-Uncle of 201 Squadron.

Right: BETWEEN-FLIGHTS-CHECK. NM-V N9029 of 228 Squadron has a brief external check-over at Alexandria between rescue missions, 1941.

Above: Another view of NM-X 228 Squadron, patiently waiting for a 'load' off Greece, 1941. In foreground, bottom, can just be seen the VGO barrels and metal cupola shields of the mid-upper gun hatches of a sister Sunderland.

Above right: REPAIR BASE. Syriam, home of 346 Wing (located at the Burman Oil Facility) which serviced Sunderlands and Catalinas detached to Rangoon from Ceylon. In background is the river Pegu and the promontory known as Monkey Point, at the junction of the Rangoon River.

Far right: Syriam Pier, leading out over the River Pegu. In centre background ise a 230 Squadron Sunderland.

luck was in and he reached Suda Bay without mishap. Meanwhile Sunderlands U and V of 230 Squadron complemented by the BOAC C-Class 'boats *Cambria* and *Coorong*, lifted 127 men from Suda to Alexandria. The skipper (D K Bednall) of Sunderland Y/230 attempted to follow from Suda with only three engines operating — the propeller of the fourth having been crudely lashed with rope. The temporary lashing soon worked loose and Bednall alighted in a sheltered bay south of Crete. The offending starboard inner engine's prop was restrapped more securely and Bednall completed his trip to Alexandria without further trouble. April 25th saw Alex Frame rescue a Group Captain and 50 RAF men from Kalamata; while Flight Lieutenant Harry Lamond of 228 Squadron, skippering Sunderland T9084, was sent to the Githeron area to lift a party of RAF men reported there. Signalled by hand-mirrors from the nearby shore, Lamond landed and anchored about 100 yards out. The RAF party, 130 men under the command of Flight Lieutenant Magner of 112 Squadron, was contacted and

52 of these were taken aboard and flown back to Suda Bay. He had promised to return at 20·00 hours to pick up another batch of the 112 Squadron party but events changed this intention — and Lamond's immediate future. In his own words, '. . . In the afternoon I was sent to Kalamata where a whole host of army and a few RAF were assembling as it was the last bit of Greece they could get to. I didn't have all that much fuel on board and calculated that we would be all right with 80 and took on that number (I believe they were counted off as 82!) That made 92 on board with the crew. But it was no trouble to T9048 and she took off like a bird. We arranged them (the passengers) from the front turret back to the end of the step and she balanced out almost dead right. I was being refuelled for an op the next day when the refuelling was stopped and I was ordered off for the third trip that day to do a night trip to Kalamata — without a flare path either end. I had to take a message — about Navy plans to mount an evacuation exercise I believe, though I was not told that. The take-off was

hair-raising as there were plenty of sunken ships in Suda Bay with bits above water, but it was dark and misty and much too calm at Kalamata for landing using only the landing light. We had some trouble finding our way there, but I didn't have enough fuel to hang about for daylight and I couldn't land back at Suda, so land at Kalamata it had to be. I never saw the surface — and poor old T9048 tore out her nose plates and turned over. The fuselage was torn away from the wing and those of us who survived found refuge on the wing which was floating upside down with the floats sticking straight up. There were four of us but one was uninjured and was able to get away on a surface craft the next day with other RAF personnel. I was not too bad myself but stayed to see if I could get the other two who were badly injured onto any hospital boat that might come in. Unfortunately the Germans arrived first — during the night — and I finished up as the only RAF officer prisoner of war with some thousands of army types.'

On April 26th, the day after Lamond's

Flight Lieutenant J Rand, from Bishop Auckland (left) and Flight Sergeant F Wright prepare to take-off from Calcutta in Sunderland 'O' for their mercy detachment

DEPOT. A typical scene at
the main flying boat
servicing base of Koggala,
Ceylon — the maintenance
centre for Sunderlands and
Catalinas during the last
three years of the war.

Tropical troubles

Nigel Argent joined 270 Squadron at Apapa, Lagos on October 1st, 1944, and for the next eight months had a wide variety of experiences in Sunderlands, though mainly in the 'non-operational' sphere — a circumstance of the location and lack of enemy activity there. If he and his fellow Sunderland crews lacked excitement in the more accepted sense of 'operations', they certainly had no hum-drum, backwater war. Operating a flying boat in the tropics meant flying in conditions which called for a cool head, steady nerves, and an ability to adapt quickly to a broad range of totally unexpected dangers. The following extracts from a diary he kept illustrate only too well that the Japanese and German enemies were by no means the only hazards.

'On December 30, 1944, I went with Flt Lt Thomson (in DW109,Q) to Libreville. We took a varied lot of passengers and I was navigating (my first nav trip in a Sunderland, and part of my working-up to a captain's course). The journey was uneventful, but I was somewhat alarmed to see the hill up which the trucks had to climb to camp. The road journey (to the camp) took an hour over a very rough road and one stream which was crossed by raft, propelled by natives. After a boxing competition, at midnight the dancing began and we felt it was time to get back.

However, we did not get away until three am. Next day we set off for Pointe Noire, three hours' flying away. We were within 25 miles of P.N. when thunderstorms forced us out to sea and we attempted to go round to the south. Eventually we had to send out a signal 'fuel remaining for one hour' and began to jettison ammo, guns and pyrotechnics, but not our own luggage (nor the wine demi-johns we were taking to get refilled at P.N. . . .) By this time we'd been forced out to sea 100 miles, and it did not seem a good place to ditch. Accordingly we made straight for the coast through all the storms and eventually came out by Lake M'Banio on which we landed after three hours in storms. Jimmy Thomson and Fg Off Trevor Hughes did a grand job of piloting in spite of a flooded cockpit — both were wearing mackintoshes as the windows leaked so much. We could not find winds, but Larry Pennell and I kept an air plot of the 24 alterations of course in 1½ hours, and our guessed DR position was about 20 miles too near the coast. Once on the lake (which was about 20 miles long by three wide and very deep) we anchored about 300 yards from shore and took stock of our position. We had not much food, but an Anson soon flew over and dropped a message telling of a food dump 20 miles away at Mayumba. I paddled out in

Left: ML868, a Mk III of 230 Squadron, over-flying Koggala Lake, Ceylon.

Below: CRYSTAL SEAS. EJ143 of 230 Squadron raising a neat plume on take-off from the coral island base at Diego Garcia in the Indian Ocean, after a refuelling stopover.

**Above: BLACK PETER.
The unique all-black
Sunderland (JM673)
'owned' by Wing
Commander D K Bednall,
then commander of 230
Squadron. The idea of the
funereal finish was for
participation in dawn/dusk
attacks on coastal shipping
in the Bay of Bengal.**

**Right: BLACK AND
WHITE. 'Black Peter'
(JM673), piloted by the OC
230 Squadron, Wg Cdr D K
Bednalll leading two all-
white Sunderlands of the
same unit ('J' &'H') on his
farewell 'parade' on
relinquishing command of
230.**

a K-type dinghy to pick up the message in a tin. Various native canoes soon visited us with eggs and pineapples and unripe bananas. That night was not comfortable, and we did not consider Horlicks tablets and tea the right way to celebrate New Year's Eve — but after all we might well have been in dinghies in the open sea!

Next day we expected food and fuel early, but we only saw the Anson again at mid-day and were told to expect supplies about 3 pm. Meanwhile we paddled around in the D-type dinghy and visited the shore. (Larry Pennell even went off in a native canoe to visit the native villages). At 3 pm we saw nothing of our rescue party but the engineers started work on our engines, only finishing after dark, working by the light of an Aldis lamp that I was holding. We then settled down to a well-organised night, but at 9 pm the first canoe arrived with Sqn Ldr Hordern (CO of Pointe Noire), three Frenchmen and a girl. All had to be fed and accommodated for the night. I slept in the bomb room until the petrol finally arrived at 1 am, nine 45-gallon drums of an unknown octane, in a canoe. Our APU and bilge pumps were unserviceable, so I went into the canoe and for the next 3¼ hours poured the petrol into 5-gallon water cans, which were hauled up to the deck. The engineers worked all night and then moved onto the engines to finish the DI's. At nine o'clock we took off after a very short run, and so reached P.N. safely after 42 hours waterborne. We were really none the worse for our adventures, and I really began to appreciate what a crew spirit can mean.

On March 10th, 1945, prior to a proposed

trip to Jui, we took up Sunderland H for a final air test. The aircraft had previously shown a lot of vibration and the cause could not be found — indeed, everyone thought we were inventing the trouble to avoid going to Jui. We were flying over Lagos when the port inner propeller flew off. (I was in the right-hand seat and the look of horror on the skipper's face as the prop overtook us was something to remember — did he have time to recall that this was the prop that should spin into the cockpit and kill the pilot?). This happened after about 15 minutes flight, and after noticing excessive vibration from the P.I., its flame damper shaking about quite noticeably, though little movement on the gills. After a loud bang, the prop flew forward about five feet, then crashed back into the wing leading edge, knocking the maintenance door out, and finally rebounding forward gashing a six-foot hole in the hull across the ward room and ending some nine inches above the water line. Flt Lt Russell immediately took 'George' (automatic pilot) out of control, throttled back and switched off. There was no fire in the engine and we were well placed crosswind over Lagos (into which busy area the prop fell, though it hit nobody. . .) so Russ dived for the alighting area. Speed was pushed up to 160 knots to lose height (we were at 1600 feet when the accident happened) and an immediate approach was made. Control was difficult due to bad vibration and the maintenance door being out on top of the mainplane, but a perfect landing (without flaps) was made. It was then that we discovered the full extent of the damage to the hull, and H was up the slip in no time. (Cause of the prop loss was found to be shearing of the reduction gear). Sunderland H was gradually serviced, all engines being removed, but three months later was still just an ornament. The hull was repaired just as VE Day arrived and the aircraft was launched, towed out to sea, and used for target practice by the Navy ML's — though after half an hour she had to be sunk by knocking holes in the hull. . . Incidentally, the same skipper was the only pilot to have lost a prop before, this time the starboard inner which was supposed to remove the outer with it (it was always said), and we could not fly on two with the Pegasus XVIII. Again, he was lucky — it missed!

One useful flight was made on Monday, May 21st, 1945, when at short notice we were chosen to fly Fg Off Morgan to Jui. He had been suffering from infantile paralysis for two months, and had both legs and one arm completely paralysed. At one time he developed septicaemia from prickly heat and only penicillin kept him alive. Jolts caused him pain, so we realised the importance of our job. We went off in Sunderland L, the best aircraft of the squadron. Morgan was brought alongside in a bomb scow and loaded through the bomb doors into the bomb room where a hospital bed had been arranged. Accompanying him were Flt Lt Henson, our squadron MO, and an army nursing sister. Fg Off Collins was to accompany us in aircraft K. We climbed straight up to 600 feet and maintained a ground speed of about 145 knots. All the way to Cape Palmas it was grand, but then the clouds rose too high and we had to come down. It became hot and bumpy and very unpleasant for our patient. However, we were waterborne after 9¼ hours and there was a bomb scow ready. The original idea had been for an aircraft to fly Morgan all the way, but this was squashed by AHQ who said he was to go on a ship from Freetown — disappointing for us as this was after VE-Day and we were to return home soon anyway. When we arrived we were told that he was to go 15 miles by mountain road to hospital and would only go aboard ship next day. Henson refused to let him be moved and eventually permission was got for him to go down to Freetown by pinnace. Even then he went through hell of a time and only got to bed at 8 pm after being up at 4.30 am. Next day he went safely aboard the *Mauretania* and we heard no more about his journey. Now we were concerned about getting back to Apapa as we found everyone at Jui agog with the news that all squadrons on the coast were to move back to the UK. First we were given orders to fly to Port Etienne, and next morning we were up at dawn and had a very pleasant trip to P.E., passing Dakar on the way. Port Etienne is just a spit of sand sticking out from the desert, and the RAF camp consists of Nissen huts. We landed some way out to sea and had quite a rough taxi in to the moorings (we had gone to pick up Flt Lt Powell who was sick and could not leave). So we refuelled and most of the crew slept aboard the aircraft. Again we were off at first light and had a much quicker journey back to Jui — 14½ hours flying, and probably 2500 gallons of petrol, all for nothing. 'L' was behaving grandly and we were purring along with low rpm, low fuel consumption and 120 knots, with Colin Jeffery at the controls. We were conscious that we could now be three-

quarters of the way to the UK, but the final leg back to Lagos showed that it was a good thing that our patient was not still with us.

For the third morning running we went off at dawn. The weather was very thundery and we went through a lot of rain. After four and a half hours' flying we were forced to make for Abidjan as the starboard inner engine began cutting and, altogether, cut about 12 times in the next hour. After landing at Abidjan we found that we had used some 13 gallons of oil in the engine, and suspected that the oil was getting through to the bottom cylinders. However, we thought we could make it to Apapa and, next morning, set off again. After only 20 minutes flying we were ordered back to Abidjan as weather was u/s at Apapa. Directly we turned back the starboard inner began cutting again. After landing back at Abidjan, we found that the piston rings had gone on No. 6 cylinder — one of the bottom ones and the worst to

change. We had a spare cylinder but no new pistons and few correct tools. Nevertheless, the two engineers and a few of us helping set to work to get the old 'pot' off, having sent a signal off requesting spares. By that night the old pot was nearly off. We were moored close to the shore, but preferred to use a rowing boat rather than the motor dinghies as then we were more independent. Next day the cylinder was off but there was no sign of our spare piston from Apapa. Early the following day Fg Off Dunn arrived with the necessary equipment and maintenance staff, and brought cigarettes and chocolate, though he forgot our mail. By noon on Tuesday we had a successful taxi test and were ready to go. One of the worst jobs over the long stay was cleaning out the galley bilges. After living aboard for so long, a certain amount of stuff had got into the bilges and they were getting a little 'high' — one drawback to flying boats. . .

Above left: ENGINE TROUBLE. JM671, Z-Zebra of 95 Squadron forced to ditch near Bathurst with power problems, 1944.

Left: Half Die Camp, Bathurst, 1941 — the base for 204 Squadron at that time. Beyond the trees in the back ground was Marina Camp, right on the beach-line.

Above: Servicing a Sunderland at Red Hills, Madras State in June 1945 — another main servicing depot for flying boats.

Peace and Goodwill

CARGO QUEEN. GR5, VB 889, NS-D of 201 Squadron on the Havel Lake, Berlin during Operation Plainfare (the Berlin Air Lift, 1948). This was last Blackburn–built Sunderland, and first flew on November 8th, 1945. It was transferred in 1948 from 201 Squadron to 235 OCU, Calshot, as TA-K, and was still on charge at Calshot in 1954.

Below: TIGHT TRIO. Tfhree 201 Squadron GR5's etch a triple wake across the waters of Milford Haven, just after the war.

Inset far left: Sunderland GR5's of 201 Squadron flying over London in the 1946 Victory Fly-Past celebrations. Leading is VB881, NS-A, which later became NZ4112 of the RNZAF.

Left: MOTLEY MIXTURE. An aerial view of the Sunderland base at Calshot, Hampshire in 1948, depicting Sunderlands of the three main units based there at the time — 201 Squadron (NS-), 230 Squadron (4X-), and 235 OCU (TA-). In foreground is Calshot Castle, the centuries-old landmark (often mistakenly referred to as a Martello tower) which housed the radio, radar and air traffic control sections.

Above right: TRAINER. GR5, NJ205, TA-F of 235 OCU, Calshot, 1948, moored on the Solent River. This aircraft later became Short Solent 3, G-AKNS, 'City of Liverpool' with BOAC, and was finally scrapped at Hamworthy in 1954.

Below right: DP198 of 201 Squadron resting on the Thames near the Tower of London, on September 11th, 1956, skippered by Flight Lieutenant Nicoll, which participated in that week's Battle of Britain Memorial Fly-Past over London.

Below: RN288 of 235 OCU, Calshot, 1948, moored in the Solent.

Left: TWO QUEENS. Sunderland GR5, ML763, P9-Q of the Anti-Submarine Warfare Development Unit (ASWDU), Calshot, beached on a Calshot slipway as RMS *Queen Elizabeth* heads down the Solent towards the open sea.

Below: Kowloon Bay scene, 1955, with an 88 Squadron Sunderland.

Right: An excellent prospect of GR5, RN284 of 201 Squadron. Above the side hatch door is the squadron badge. In 1946-47, this aircraft served as 'C' in 201 Squadron.

Far right, top: RECCE. Flying Officer Brand and crew climb aboard C-Charlie of 88 Squadron, 1950, prior to a reconnaissance over Korea's Yellow Sea coast.

Below: D-Dog of 201 Squadron (VB889) landing on Britannia Lake, August 1953, during support operations for the British North Greenland Expedition there — just one more example of the myriad peacetime operations undertaken by the ubiquitous Sunderlands.

Below right: PP117, 4X-W, a GR5 of 230 Squadron — a superb view of the sleek Sunderland lines.

147

TAKE-OFF. JM718 gets
airborne. In March 1953 it
was at Calshot, on strength
of 235 OCU.

Left: FORMATION
STUFF. Four of 201
Squadron's Sunderlands
return in triumph to
Pembroke Dock in August
1954, bringing home the
British North Greenland
Expedition after its two
years' sojourn.

Below: PP122, 'E' of 201
Squadron which hit a
submerged rock landing at
St Peter Port, Guernsey on
September 15th, 1954. While
the tide is out, ground crew
are using cement to repair a
30-feet gash in the hull.
Formerly P9-S of the
ASWDU, Calshot, this
aircraft was also O-Orange
of 201 Squadron for a
period.

Unique head-on view of two Sunderlands from the 'linked' 205/209 Squadron at Seletar, Singapore, taken by Master Engineer V M Reeve during an air/sea exercise 'Monsoon' over the central China Sea, 1956.

Swansong

BOAC's G-AGHV, 'Hamble' (ex-JM722) in immediate postwar livery gets away. It eventually capsized and was lost on the night of March 9/10th, 1946.

154

Above left: CIVIL EYRIE. The Hythe base in Hampshire, showing the (then) new mooring jetty and one of the floating jetties Centre right is the long-used ferry jetty for passengers crossing the Solent to Southampton.

Above: KIWI. Sunderland GR5, NZ4113, ex-PP124.

Left: DINGHIES AND DOLLIES. The beginning of civil use of Sunderlands, a scene at Poole, Dorset in September 1943.

Far left: CIVIL WARRIOR. Sunderland III, G-AGKY, 'Hungerford' passing over the Gizeh pyramids, just south of Cairo, Egypt. Formerly ML789, it sank off Calshot on January 28th, 1953, was salvaged but then scrapped in May 1953.

Above right:
CONVERSION. NJ201 in unarmed and much modified state as loaned to RAF Transport Command, coded OZZA, for trials. It then went to BOAC as G-AGWU.

Above: Short Solent 3, G-AKNU, 'Sydney' in the livery of Aquila Airways. Ex-NJ207, it finally crashed at Chessell Down, Isle of Wight on November 15th, 1957.

Below: IN SHEEP'S CLOTHING. Short Sandringham 5, G-AHZA, 'Penzance'. During the war it had been '3-H' of 423 Squadron RCAF; then became 'H' of 201 Squadron and on April 30th, 1945 was skippered by Flight Lieutenant K Foster when he shared in the destruction of U-325. It was eventually scrapped at Hamworthy, Dorset in March 1959.

GR5, ML778, NS-Z of 201 Squadron which, skippered by Wg Cdr J Barrett, DFC (of *Kensington Court* fame) flew the ultimate official convoy escort patrol of the war on June 3/4th, 1945. This view of Z-Zebra hugging the waves close to its wards exemplifies the ever-present protection afforded by Sunderlands from the first to the last day of hostilities.

Finale

Photo Credits